The
Upside
150 Uplifting Devotions

ALLEN CHAPIN

ALLEN CHAPIN

ISBN:
ISBN-13: 9781731097996

DEDICATION

This book is dedicated to my parents,
the youth pastors,
the professors,
and the other spiritual leaders in my life
who taught me the value of
spending time alone with the Lord daily.
My walk with Him today is
a direct result of you teaching me
this one, life-transforming
spiritual discipline.

CONTENTS

ACKNOWLEDGMENTS

I'd like to thank the following people for their investment in giving this book an Upside...

- *Angela, Alex and Austin… for loving me and inspiring me with your stories and your own time alone with the Lord each day.*
- *Dad and Mom… for training up this child in the way he should go so that when I was older I would not depart from it.*
- *David Wilson… for holding me accountable to my TAWG so that I would understand how deeply essential, important and special it is*
- *Jessica Horton… for once again editing with excellence and showing me how this book could have even more of an Upside.*
- *Chris Deville… for making the cover design look so great that people would be willing to give this book a chance.. and thereby discover the Upside.*
- *And most importantly, the Lord… for meeting me each day, drawing me closer to You in our times together, showing me the Upside of life lived daily with You, and giving me this opportunity to write.*

ALLEN CHAPIN

INTRODUCTION

Another daily devotional? Why? Haven't these been
written for hundreds of years? Aren't there enough out there for
people to choose from? Why produce one more?

Well, for me, it came down to these two main reasons...

First, I wanted to offer a faith-filled, positive, upbeat, encouraging, motivating devotional which comes at our daily relationship with the Lord in a way that doesn't beat people down,
but instead builds people up.

And second, one of the greatest lessons I have learned
over the years is the importance of a fresh, daily, one-on-one,
personal relationship with the Lord.

Growing up, our family had family devotions together
until I was probably midway through my teen years. Each morning, we would all trickle into that small kitchen with its minimal
dining area. I can still see the harvest gold, avocado, and mostly
burnt orange color scheme in which the room was decorated.
Mom would be putting food on the table for us, or telling us what
options were available for us to fix our own breakfast. I had a lot
of Pop-Tarts, Captain Crunch, and Cocoa Puffs during those
years. We would drag in, taking our normal seats on the wooden
bench or in one of the wooden chairs around that breakfast area
table. Then Dad would start the devotion.

Sometimes it was a Psalm. Often it was the chapter of
the day in Proverbs. (Proverbs has 31 chapters filled with practi-

cal, how-to-live concepts from a father to his kids. So it was a good fit.)

But I vividly recall one season of those family devotions which I enjoyed more than any other. Mom and Dad had bought the family a small, paperback boxed-set edition of seven books by a guy named C.S. Lewis, called, *The Chronicles of Narnia*. I found myself captivated, mesmerized each morning as Dad read the on-going adventures of Peter, Edmund, Susan and Lucy with Aslan. Dad would read a chapter and ask us what we thought it meant. Then we would peel apart the layers of the allegory as it related to our life of following Jesus, like we were some kind of tight-knit, geeked-out book club.

Stream forward through the years to my college days. I had the amazing privilege of being able to attend a Christian university which had chapel services five days per week, began each class with prayer, and had a weekly devotion time on each dormitory hall. And while we didn't always appreciate it, the school also required us to attend church on Sunday mornings. That's a lot of spiritual intake. So, if my time alone with the Lord each day was inconsistent during that time, it didn't seem to have a massive impact on me because I was being spoon-fed spiritually on a daily basis.

Then I graduated, got married, and began my first full-time ministry role. Now I was only getting spiritually nurtured Sunday mornings and evenings. On top of that, I was beginning to pour out spiritually to others on a regular basis. Before I knew it, I found myself starving spiritually.

All that changed early one morning, when I woke up before Angela, and went into the living room to have my coffee and read the Bible. I sat down in the La-Z-Boy recliner, sipped that warm nectar of heaven, and ate spiritually. While I digested the Word of God that morning, He spoke. Not audibly, but quietly to my spirit. He told me that if I would meet Him each morning like that, He would be there waiting to have coffee with me. Obviously, God didn't show up physically in my living room and sip a cup of joe with me. I knew what He meant. He was offering friendship… relationship… intimacy.

THE UPSIDE

I decided to take Him up on His offer, and I have not regretted making that decision. In fact, I would say that it has become the single biggest difference-maker in my relationship with the Lord. For more than two decades, I've been meeting alone with Him in the morning. I still sit in a recliner and sip coffee while we talk… while I read His Word… while I try to get to know Him as a well as He knows me.

I'm not saying I've had a perfect record, never missing a day. Nor am I suggesting that every day is like heaven on earth during that time alone with Him. I'm simply saying that I wouldn't trade that time with Him for anything else.

Just like I can't claim I'm starving when there is food in abundance at my disposal which I simply choose not to eat, neither can I only go to church for one service on Sunday, hear one 30-minute sermon from God's Word, sing songs of worship for just 20 minutes, pray one or two prayers, and then complain that I don't get fed spiritually when I actually have access to God every day... if I will simply make time for Him.

One of the most crucial disciplines I was ever taught was to spend time daily connecting with God through His Word, through conversation with Him and through letting Him know how much He means to me. This is actually a huge portion of what makes up our daily walk with the Lord.

Over more than two decades in ministry, I have probably beat this drum more than any other. Those who learn this discipline usually turn out to be stronger in their faith. Those who determine it isn't that important for them usually end up struggling in their walk with the Lord.

Time spent alone with the Lord each day doesn't have to be lengthy. It doesn't have to be deep or difficult. It just has to be real and meaningful. Consistent. A priority.

Since having a daily, personal, fresh, one-on-one time alone with the Lord is so vitally important to a believer's improving relationship with Him, when I began to write books, I was determined that I would make sure to write some that would help people in this area of their lives. To that end, I have written these brief devotions with real stories and thoughts from my life and the lives of others. Along with each devotion, I've included a portion of Scripture. If you don't have time that day for the whole passage, I've even given you a key verse from that passage to focus on. And, if you aren't really sure how to talk with God, I have given you a short, 2-3 sentence prayer starter to help get the conversation started on that topic.

What I'm talking about is not a duty. This is not a chore. It's also not something to simply check off our to-do list. It is the art of disciplining ourselves to get something we truly want and need. We discipline ourselves by exercising our bodies in order to be healthy and look fit... to achieve a goal. In the same way, the goal of this spiritual discipline is to grow closer in our relationship with the Lord and be spiritually stronger. In time, discipline will turn duty into delight.

My hope and prayer is that you will commit today to taking these next several months to build an enjoyable, encouraging daily time alone with the Lord. If you will apply yourself to draw close to God in a genuine way, I promise you based on His Word, that God will connect with you, and your relationship with Him will begin to have a new *Upside*. If you will choose a time and place to meet alone with Him, you will find that He will be right there waiting for you when you arrive each day.

In fact, let's take a moment right now and commit ourselves to this new endeavor of enjoyment in our relationship with the Lord...

Heavenly Father, thank You for loving us so much that You want to be with us... Immanuel. Thank You for making a way through the sacrifice of Your Son, Jesus, for us to come to you at any time with confidence as Your children. We commit ourselves to not just the next several months spent using this book, but to a lifetime of getting to know You more deeply in order to draw closer to You so that when we one day greet You in Heaven, it will be as best of friends... and not merely as acquaintances! We love You! Amen.

THE UPSIDE

DAY 1
MY SIMPLE GOAL

I noticed again as I ran errands yesterday how few people smile in public. It so stood out to me that I began to smile on purpose. I pretended I was walking down main street in a small town, greeting everyone as if I knew them personally. But few people smiled back.

I wondered... Why can't we just smile? I mean, as Christians, we claim to be full of joy. Well, where is it? How about simply curving those lips upward regularly throughout each day and letting a little of that joy slip out to others?

I don't need to make new year's resolutions. I don't need to write out a list of goals I plan to achieve. I don't need to hire a life coach. (At least I don't think I just for this.)

No, I am simply determined to do one thing well. To be kind. To be thoughtful. To speak encouraging words. To give. Sometimes just to smile... so that anyone I encounter can see the love, joy, and peace of Jesus inside me. That's it. I plan to smile.

But maybe you've just had a pretty rough year. A loved one got diagnosed with a serious disease... or maybe you did. Or perhaps you lost your job. Or your marriage struggled. And maybe some days it feels difficult to even force a smile.

Don't give up. Scripture says, "...the joy of the Lord is your strength!" That means you can both have that joy and share that joy. Hang in there!

And find your niche. Maybe it's secretly blessing people financially. Maybe it's writing more thank you notes. Maybe it's choosing to post only positive, uplifting thoughts on social media. Or maybe it's simply smiling as much as you possibly can every day. Just set one simple goal, and go for it.

Scripture To Study: Nehemiah 8:1-13
Key Verse: "...the joy of the Lord is your strength!"
Prayer: *Heavenly Father, please help me this year to daily reach my one simple goal of regularly blessing others in some small way. Remind me that my ability to bless them does not come from my circumstances, but it comes from all the ways you bless me daily. I love You, and...*

DAY 2
UNCLOGGED DRAIN

Wits end. That's where I was. I had poured drain cleaner down the kitchen sink... repeatedly. I had snaked it with a manual snake and a drill-powered snake, but nothing I tried had worked. The sink would take hours to drain. Not wanting to wash anymore dishes in the bathroom sink, we decided to call a plumber. Within a couple hours, Jerry showed up to help us.

Jerry shot water through our pipes at 4,500 PSI and six GPM three times before he finally got them unclogged. What came up in our sinks as he forced the clog backward was a black sludge made up of grease and dirt. Jerry said that it usually only takes one shot to clean out most drains. Twice, and it's pretty bad. He could hardly believe he had to do it three times on ours. As we wrapped up the business, he told me these drains had probably never been cleaned out.

Think about that... a 40-year old house that has never had the drains cleaned out. Jerry said that if we have problems in the future, we should call for help at the first sign of trouble.

That Jerry is a pretty smart guy. It's easy for us to let things build up in our lives instead of getting them cleaned out. We throw minor efforts at dealing with them, but they remain.

David called out for help in Psalm 51 when he said, "Create in me a clean heart, O God, and renew a right spirit in me." In other words, clean out my drain pipes, Lord, so that no sludge stays in there. Blow out un-forgiveness, bad attitudes, and wrong thoughts. Clear the line so that Your Holy Spirit is free to flow through me and bless others.

Call on God today to do some spiritual plumbing clean-out in our lives. Don't wait and make it any tougher. Do it now.

Scripture To Study: Psalm 51:1-19
Key Verse: "Create in me a clean heart, O God. Renew a loyal spirit within me."
Prayer: *Lord, please clean out my heart and mind today. Wash out all the sludge-like feelings and thoughts which are clogging up my life and keeping You from flowing freely through me. And please help me keep my heart and mind cleaned out regularly. I love You, and...*

DAY 3
CHEERLEADERS

My niece, Shelby, is a major superstar cheerleader. She cheers with a squad that competes on the national and world levels. On top of that, she has a great attitude and is not stuck on herself. She also happens to be brilliant and has a terrific life-plan laid out. So cheering isn't the only thing she good at, but still she is a fantastic cheerleader.

My sweet wife, Angela, is *my* biggest cheerleader. She is always right there with me. Believing in me. Encouraging me. Stirring my hope and faith. Doing what it takes to keep me going toward my goals.

If I've just mowed, she tells me how great the yard looks. If I'm just about to preach a message to a crowd in a setting I'm nervous about, she tells me I will hit it out of the park. If I actually put my dishes in the dishwasher, she takes note of it and commends me.

We all need someone in our life like that... someone who is our biggest cheerleader. We need an encourager who believes in us when no one else believes in us. And I believe God uses people to be His voice cheering others on. To be His fist-bump or high-five. His "Go get 'em, champ!"

In Scripture, Saul had just converted to Christianity, but no one believed him because he had most recently been having Christians imprisoned and killed. He needed a cheerleader. So, God gave Saul Barnabas. Whatever he said to the others worked, because the Christians soon accepted Saul and began to support his missionary endeavors.

Who could say that you are their biggest cheerleader? Why don't you take time right now to pick one person and determine to cheer them on ridiculously? I mean, go over the top. Embarrass them with your cheering. Then watch as that person begins to become all they dream of becoming.

Scripture To Study: Acts 9:19-30
Key Verse: "Then Barnabas brought him to the apostles..."
Prayer: *Lord, I want to encourage others and cheer them on in the way You would. Please help me to see those around me whom I can encourage. And help me cheer them on like crazy so that they can accomplish all You have planned for them in life. I love You, and...*

DAY 4
THE BLESSING OF BUMPERS

Our church had a family fun night at a small, local bowling alley. PR31 (aka, Angela) and I ended up on a lane with our boys and some of the other younger kids. We quickly realized we needed bumpers on our lane. Bumpers are those pieces of foam that bowling alley employees slide down the gutters so that kids cannot miss, but instead knock down pins with every try.

With bumpers in place, all the kids on our lane started having more fun. The rules of the game didn't change at all. Had they rolled a gutter ball (in those last 3 feet without bumpers), they still would have scored zero for that roll. They still had to stand the same distance from the pins. They still had to roll heavy balls with three holes.

Now, though, they were able to accomplish what was impossible before. The bumpers made it possible and gave them a sense of anticipation and joy in each roll. Their balls zigged and zagged down that lane, but they scored every time because of the bumpers.

Now, let's be honest... None of us are very proficient at keeping God's rules. In fact, the Apostle Paul writes to the believers in the church at Rome, saying none of us match up to God's standard. We roll gutter balls pretty regularly when it comes to being and doing all that God expects of those who have things squared with Him.

Yet the rules don't change. So I'm glad that God offered to put bumpers in the lane of life for us. Since we cannot keep all of God's rules in order to stay right with Him, Jesus came to make it possible for us. So it is His grace which brings joy to life for us. We can look forward to each effort at serving Him because we know we are going to win.

Some people want to try to do it on their own, but I'll take a strike with a bumper over a gutter ball without it every day!

Scripture To Study: Romans 3:21-31
Key Verse: "...we all fall short of God's glorious standard."
Prayer: *Heavenly Father, thank You for putting the bumpers of Your grace in my life so that I could be right with You. I cannot win on my own. I need Your grace. I choose to put my faith in Jesus instead of my own ability to get life right. I love You, and...*

DAY 5
LIFE HACK FOR SUCCESS

Whether you are a stay-at-home wife or mom trying to tackle a mountain of laundry. Or a business leader assigned an incredibly important project. Or a politician trying to get legislation passed. Or a preacher working on a weekly sermon. Maybe a military leader assigned with covertly defeating an enemy force. Or a student writing an essay. We all want to succeed. We want to make good grades. Or get a promotion. Or make a difference. Or even just check one more thing off a nagging to-do list. Yet success seems so elusive at times.

But don't give up hope. Between watching Special Agent OSO with my boys when they were younger and a trip I took to Israel where we met with a former Israeli Defense Force (IDF) leader, I have discovered that any task can be completed much more easily, with less stress, if I will do just one thing...

What is this God-designed life hack for success? Break any task, project or assignment into three steps. This is what the IDF does with everything they do. By breaking tasks into three steps or parts, it:

- creates a clearer sense of what needs to be accomplished
- speeds up the process
- makes assigning tasks easier
- breaks the giant into bite-sized chunks

If the three steps still seem too big, then break each one of them into three steps. This will work with practically anything you need to accomplish. Success is just three steps away. And remember these powerful words of encouragement from Tony Little... "Yeah, baby, you can do it!"

Scripture To Study: Genesis 6:9-22
Key Verse: "Build a large boat... waterproof it... Then construct decks and stalls..."
Prayer: *Dear God, I have a lot of work to get done, and I need Your wisdom. Please help me see the simplest way to break down my tasks into three bite-sized chunks. I want to accomplish all I am supposed to so that I can honor You with my life. Thank You for helping me! I love You, and...*

DAY 6
WHO'S MAKING YOUR SUPPER?

It's a simple concept which I choose to live by. You don't have to wonder what I mean when I say something because I say what I mean, and I mean what I say. So, when it comes down to a simple-living tip we could all use, I like this one... "If I didn't have to do it, then I don't get to complain."

It's best illustrated by who's cooking at our house. PR31 basically does all the cooking. She wants to make sure what she cooks for us is just right. When she is forced to serve something she is not completely pleased with, she offers an apology for the bacon being too crisp or the cookies being a little underdone in the middle, etc. Without fail, my response to her apology is a question...

Me: Hey, did I have to make it?

PR31: Well, no, but...

Me: (interrupting) Hey, if I didn't have to make it, then I don't get to complain.

PR31: Yeahhhh... I hear ya, boy.

I don't just apply this principle to meals cooked by my sweetheart or other acts of kindness by others toward me. I apply it to my salvation.

I didn't pay for my rescue from hell. I didn't earn my adoption into God's family. I didn't work hard enough for God to bless me so abundantly. God did it. So I don't get to complain when He gives me some guidelines to live by, and asks me to do something that takes me out of my comfort zone, or challenges me to new levels of excellence.

What if we each chose to complain less and appreciate more? Give it a try today with God... and with others.

Scripture To Study: Ephesians 2:1-10
Key Verse: "Salvation is not a reward for the good things we have done, so none of us can boast..."
Prayer: *Lord, thank You for everything You have done... are doing... and will do for me. I know I didn't earn my way into Your family, and I am forever grateful. I choose to appreciate You rather than complain today, regardless of what You ask of me. I love You, and...*

DAY 7
SCOUTING PROSPECTS

A couple of years ago, I was talking with The Lord about our two boys and about how I believe in their significant potential. As I addressed the topic with Him, I sensed the Lord stun me with this challenge to my heart and mind, "*Discover your children.*"

It so took me off-guard that I was lost in the thought for a moment. Then, it was as if the thought continued and I sensed Him explain... "*Allen, there are people in this world who are searching to discover others. There are scouts looking for the next great sports star, singer, the next standout CEO, the next great actor, or artist, or author, or chef, or political leader.*"

The Lord went on to challenge me that morning to be the one to discover our boys... to discover their talents, skills, personalities, aptitudes, abilities, and strengths. I'm not suppose to delegate that responsibility to someone else, or allow any random person in this world of scouting potential to beat me to the punch with my own boys.

It's a privilege to get to be in on the spotting of potential in a person. Proverbs 22:29 asks the question, "*Do you see someone skilled in their work?*" It's not a trick question. It's simple and straightforward. Yet it does beg another question... Are you looking for potential in the people in your life? Are you on the hunt for greatness in others?

Scouts are rarely thought about or talked about. It is the superstars they discover who shine brightly for everyone to see. But those stars would never be seen if someone had not pointed them out. And there are people around you who need you to discover them as well so that they can shine. Will you keep your eyes open for them today?

Scripture To Study: Proverbs 22
Key Verse: "Do you see any truly competent workers?"
Prayer: *Dear Lord, please help me today to take my focus off of my own life and keep my eyes open for others. I want to help someone else become more of who You created them to be. Help me to see potential in people, and encourage them toward that potential. I love You, and...*

DAY 8
ALL CALLS ACCEPTED

The smartphone chirps its latest ringtone. We pick it up, turn it over and look at the screen. In that moment, we decide if we want to hit "accept" or "decline."

Admit it. There *are* people whose calls you answer immediately when you see their name on the screen. You light up inside when their name, number, and picture show up on your phone. Then there are others who cause you to pause and assess if you have the emotional strength to talk at that moment.

One night, I sat in as a helper for the kids Bible study at our church. They were learning the basics about prayer. One of those basics is that God is always listening. He always "accepts our call."

Some people think they have been too bad in life for God to accept their call, but He does. Others who really are trying to do right in life, but don't get everything perfect, have a tough time believing that God would take their call. The truth is, God has more than seven billion people in His "favorites" right now, with room for more to be added. He lights up when He sees your face on the screen.

And God never has to choose between. He takes the sinner's call for mercy while taking the saint's call for provision. God never declines our calls. And God is never too busy to take our calls. Psalm 138:3 points out that when we call, God answers. Every time.

Even though Daniel's prayer was delayed for three weeks, the angel with the answer informed him that God took his call right away.

God's not ignoring your call. He's not too busy. He delights in talking with you. Choose today to believe that God loves you, God hears you, and God will respond to you.

Scripture To Study: Psalm 116
Key Verse: "I love the Lord because He hears my voice and my prayer for mercy."
Prayer: *Heavenly Father, thank You for always taking my call when I pray. Thank You for loving me, listening to me, and responding to me. I know that I can always trust You to hear my heart and my words. I love You, and…*

DAY 9
CARING OR JUST CURIOUS?

I pulled into the junior high school's parking lot to watch the motivational assembly. I was supposed to help set up and spend some time hanging out, but I didn't help set up that day, and I didn't get to spend much time with them. When I pulled into the parking lot, I saw smoke coming from under the hood of our minivan. I popped the hood latch and found a busted radiator hose making a mess.

Enter Joe. Joe is the maintenance guy at the school. He's also an ardent follower of Christ. How do I know? Well, he told me how Christ had changed his life and how he loved sharing Jesus with as many people as possible, but I really knew because he stopped everything he was doing to help me find and fix the problem. Others asked if everything was okay. Joe kept working on my vehicle. Joe wasn't just curious... Joe cared.

Joe was not the only one who showed they cared that day. Two pastor friends hauled me to auto parts stores looking for the part I needed. When it was unavailable, one pastor offered to let me crash on his couch, drive me home or let me borrow their church van to drive myself home. I ended up not ordering the part, and instead opted for radiator stop-leak and gorilla tape to patch up the leak and drive the 45 miles home. Guess who helped me do the job right? Joe.

Jesus said people in this world would know that we are committed followers of His when we truly express our love for each other. We most resemble and exemplify God's love when we're not just curious, but when we really care for each other. Today, may we each truly express God's love for others through true caring actions!

Scripture To Study: I John 3:14-24
Key Verse: "...let's not merely say we love each other; let us show the truth by our actions."
Prayer: *Lord, I want others to know that You love them. I know I can show that love, but I need Your help today to see those around me who need Your love and help. And I need Your power and provision to help express that love so that they are drawn to You. Thank You! I love You, and...*

DAY 10
THANK THE LORD!

Recently we have noticed that our youngest son, Austin, has been saying, *"Thank the Lord"* for anything good that happens. Like all the time. And we love it!

- Made it to a new level on the video game? *"Thank the Lord!"*
- Found lint in the dryer screen to help start the burn pile? *"Thank the Lord!"*
- Mama lets him lick the bowl after making a batch of cookies? *"Thank the Lord!"*

We love that he is beginning to recognize in some small way, like Scripture says, "Every good present and every perfect gift comes from above, from the Father who made the sun, moon, and stars. The Father doesn't change like the shifting shadows produced by the sun and moon."

What if I lived more like that?

What if you did?

What if we all did?

What if, when one of us got a clearance deal at the checkout that was better than we expected, we exclaimed, *"Thank the Lord"*?

What if, when one of us got an "A" on a test, we exclaimed, *"Thank the Lord"*?

How different would the world around us become if throughout each day, we all began to declare our belief that God is the giver of good gifts?

I say we find out! Let's join Austin all throughout our days by speaking those three powerful words... *"Thank the Lord!"*

Scripture To Study: James 1:16-18

Key Verse: "Whatever is good and perfect comes down to us from God our Father..."

Prayer: *Heavenly Father, thank You for all the blessings with which You have filled my life. Thank You for the small blessings and the big blessings. Please help me to take notice of all Your abundant joys and gifts and give You thanks always. I love You, and...*

DAY 11
FOOTPRINTS ON THE MOUNTAIN

I don't know what brought you to this point. I don't know what struggles you've faced. I don't know how far you've had to climb, or how hard it was to climb. You just wonder if it's worth it. You wonder if you should give up. You wonder if you've accomplished all you are capable of accomplishing. You feel your efforts to make a difference in others have gone un-noticed. You feel small and insignificant.

But you need to know today that you were designed, destined and created for greatness. You have the skills, the knowledge, and the tools to make it. You may have already scaled heights that would cause others to shudder in fear, yet there are higher peaks ahead for you.

You weren't put on this planet to be mediocre. God has placed in you the strength, the ability, and the talent you need. He wants to come alongside you with His power to help you do more than you can imagine. He has the resources you need to make the rest of the climb.

Take a look behind you. See those footprints? Those are the ones you are leaving behind as you climb. They tell others below who wonder if they are called to greatness to keep climbing. Your good attitude, passion, consistency, relentless pursuit, joy and strength all call out to those below, "Grab hold of the line and follow my footprints. It's beautiful up here."

And know this... God loves you enough that today He intersected your life to tell you what you needed to hear. That alone should be enough to let you know that you can keep climbing. Believe me, champion, you'll look back one day in amazement at where He has brought you and be glad you did!

Scripture To Study: Romans 8:31-39
Key Verse: "No, despite all these things, overwhelming victory is ours through Christ..."
Prayer: *Lord, thank You for Your love and power. I am feeling weak today, and I need Your strength to carry me to the new heights You have up ahead of me. Please help me to be all I can be and do all I can do through You so that others can follow me as I follow You. I love You, and...*

DAY 12
THE SLOW COOKER LIFE

PR31 is a regular user of the slow cooker for our family meals. We get the boys to bed at night, and she slips into the kitchen to prep a roast, or some chicken, or a soup. Then she puts it in the slow cooker... on low... to cook overnight. When I wake up the next morning and go into the kitchen to make my coffee, I could almost gnaw my arm off because the food in that slow cooker smells so good, and I know I have to wait to get some of it till lunch.

There are times when Angela has to "rush" a meal. Maybe she forgot to put it in the slow cooker before she went to bed, and now for it to be ready by lunchtime she has to put it on the high heat setting. But she doesn't like doing that because the meat and vegetables just don't turn out the same. The juices, or gravy or soup just don't have the same flavor. Low and slow somehow seems to make things the most tender, and cause them to have the best flavor.

I wonder why we can so easily understand that food cooked in a slow cooker overnight is going to taste better and be more appealing than food nuked in a microwave for a few minutes, yet we struggle to understand that God may be trying to make something better out of us by letting us simmer in a situation for longer than we want.

If God were to rush the process in our lives, we might turn out tough and not taste as good to the world around us. Instead, He wants to work into us all the good flavors of Himself and tenderize our hearts for others before He lets us out of the holding place He has us in at the moment. If you're in a slow cooker part of life right now, I can tell you that you're in a good place. Stay put. Simmer a little. Soak up a lot of Him. Get ready to make a big impact!

Scripture To Study: Hebrews 10:32-39
Key Verse: "... Patient endurance is what you need now, so that you will continue to do God's will."
Prayer: *Heavenly Father, I don't understand why I am having to go through this right now. It's not easy, but I trust You. Thank You for Your work in my life to make me into all I can be. I love You, and...*

DAY 13
YOUR TOMORROW

I had just finished watching the inauguration of the 45th President of the United States of America, and was thinking about what a change this means for Donald J. Trump and his family. When he went to bed last night, he was still just a citizen of this nation. Tonight when he goes to bed, he will be the leader of the free world as we know it. That's quite a dramatic difference.

We, too, face moments in our lives when from one day to the next we go from one lifestyle to a completely different and elevated lifestyle.

The Apostle Paul wrote in II Corinthians 5:17, "This means that anyone who belongs to Christ has become a new person. The old life is gone; a new life has begun!" In other words, one night you go to bed as a sinner destined to split hell wide open; but after accepting Jesus Christ as your Rescuer and Friend, you go to bed the next night as a child of God. Royalty. One with new privileges and new responsibilities. One with new power and new potential.

God could do anything in your life today and totally redirect the trajectory of your life. You could go to bed tonight seeing yourself— and the world seeing you— in one light. By tomorrow night, you could go to bed seeing yourself— and being seen— in a completely different light. You could have new potential and new power. You could have new privileges and new responsibilities.

Last night, he was Donald J. Trump- businessman. Tonight, he is President Donald J. Trump- leader of the free world.

Who will you be tomorrow? Are you ready for it? What will you do when you become more than you have been?

Scripture To Study: I Kings 19:19-21
Key Verse: "...Then he went with Elijah as his assistant."
Prayer: *Lord, I know that You can change me in an instant. You saved me from my sin and adopted me into Your family in a moment's time. Please help me to be ready to be all that I can be and do all that I can do to honor You with my life as You transform me more into Your likeness. I love You, and...*

DAY 14
INFECTED AND CONTAGIOUS

The university nurse stopped by my dorm room to check on me at the request of my roommate. She took my temperature and said, "Yep, you've got a pretty high fever. Take these ibuprofen and drink lots of liquids." Then she asked, "Is there anything else?" I replied, "Well, I do have this weird rash on my chest."

"Show me," she said. So I pulled up my t-shirt and showed her the red spots polka-dotting my torso. "You have chicken pox," she said. "Get your stuff together. You're going home. You're contagious." I called my parents and gave them the news. Then I packed up all my stuff, and made the four-hour drive home.

Twenty-two years old and getting chicken pox at college was bizarre, but even more bizarre was that my Dad could not come in my room because he had shingles. The doctor told him to steer clear of me because my chicken pox could make his shingles worse.

We are all infected by those we choose to hang around. We catch their attitudes, their style of talk, and their likes and dislikes. Those who surround us, infect us. It is critically important for us to choose carefully those with whom we surround ourselves.

Additionally, you and I are not just infected by those we hang around. We have the ability to infect those who choose to hang around us. We are spreading whatever we have in us to those around us.

Who is infecting your life, and with what? Who are you infecting, and with what? Today, let's choose to be infected with all those things that are good, helpful, holy, and positive. Then let's begin to spread that to all those around us!

Scripture To Study: Numbers 13:25-14:12
Key Verse: "So they spread this bad report about the land among the Israelites:"
Prayer: *Dear Lord, I ask You to help me today to maintain a great attitude... and the same attitude as Christ Jesus. Please surround me with those whose attitudes and words build me up. Fill me with the character produced by Your Holy Spirit so that I only infect those around me with Your heart. I love You, and...*

DAY 15
DO YOU HAVE A DREAM?

Across our nation, we annually celebrate a man who had a dream to see civil rights recognized for all people. Dr. Martin Luther King, Jr. did not give up on that dream. He inspired others to dream along with him, and eventually, his dream became reality.

God has also placed dreams and desires in each of our hearts; good things for us to do which honor Him and make a positive difference in this world. Often, roadblocks keep us from those dreams.

Here are three main roadblocks which sometimes keep people from pursuing and fulfilling their dreams. I'm challenging you today to not give up on your dream because of:

- ***Time*** — It took Moses more than 40 years to get the Israelites from slavery in Egypt to their Promised Land. Joseph about 13 years to go from the pit to the palace. And Noah 120 years to build the ark that would save his family and all animal species. If God put the dream in your heart, He will bring it about regardless of how long it takes.

- ***Talk*** — People spoke against Nehemiah's dream to rebuild the wall in Jerusalem. He simply told them that he didn't have time to stop his project to talk about how they didn't believe in his dream. While others talk, just keep working that dream to make it become a reality.

- ***Trials*** — God spoke to a man named Zerubbabel, who had a dream to rebuild the temple where people could worship God, and the Lord told him that before him even a mountain in his way would become level ground. There is no challenge or obstacle which can prevent you from fulfilling the dreams God has placed in your heart.

Whatever makes you say, "I have a dream," don't give up!

Scripture To Study: Psalm 105:17-22
Key Verse: "Until the time came to fulfill his dreams, the Lord tested Joseph's character."

Prayer: *Lord, sometimes I wonder how I am ever going to become all that You have designed me to be and accomplish all You have destined me to do. I know that You will bring it all together, but I need Your strength today to stay focused on the dream You have placed in my heart. I love You, and...*

DAY 16
GARAGE SALE FINDS

I LOOOOOVVVVE a great garage sale. Okay, let's be transparent... I pretty much love any garage sale. I love going to them. I love having them. I just love garage sales. I love what they are about. It's about someone saying they don't value something enough to keep it anymore, but they value it enough to try to get someone else to pay them money for it. IT'S AWESOME!

This is where it starts to get tricky. I tend to price things a little higher. PR31 tends to price things to actually get rid of them. In the end, one of us usually asks the all important question, "If you saw it at a garage sale, how much would *you* pay for it?"

That's when it gets real. You see, if it's someone else's junk they're trying to pawn off on me, I can be extremely frugal. When it has been my own personal item, I want to sell it for a little bit more because it holds special memories...nostalgia. Yet, in the end, an item is really only worth what the buyer is willing to pay for it.

So it is a pretty amazing thought that God saw us in the garage sale pile of life, picked us up, dusted us off, looked closely, and then made an extraordinary offer. He said, "I'll give the life of my only Son to purchase this one." We weren't worth what He paid for us, but He paid it anyway because He saw something more in us than we saw in ourselves. He saw the potential of what He could transform us into.

So the next time you're at a garage sale, remember that God values you more than even you or others might value you. And let's look for that same value in others, too, because He's going to keep on looking around a little longer.

Scripture To Study: Romans 5:1-11
Key Verse: "But God showed His great love for us by sending Christ to die for us..."
Prayer: *Thank You, Lord, for finding me in the garage sale of life and choosing to purchase me. I was messed up, broken and in need of major repairs, but You paid a high price for me anyway. I am so grateful to belong to You! Please help me to live up to Your purchase price. I love You, and...*

DAY 17
LOST DOG FLASHBACK

Alex came running into our bathroom, where I was getting cleaned up to go preach somewhere. I was almost finished shaving when I turned, saw the tears in his eyes, along with the panicked look on his face, and knew something was not right in his world. When I asked what was wrong, he told me, "Sugar ran away!"

I immediately flashed back to the day when I went out to play with my dog, Pepper, only to find the gate had been left open by someone else, and she had run away. I, too, ran inside to tell my parents my dog had run away. Dad put me in the car, and we went searching, but we couldn't find her.

Several days later, Pepper turned up at the dog pound. I was overjoyed when I heard the news. We were going to have to pay money to get her back, but I didn't care. I just wanted her back.

When my eyes met Alex's, I knew what we had to do. I skipped wiping the remaining shaving cream off my top lip and told him, "Come on!" About a block up the hilly road, we came to our neighbor's house and spotted Sugar. Alex jumped out, and soon he had the escaped Sugar back in his loving arms.

I, too, was once like Pepper and Sugar. I was lost, and God came looking for me. He didn't care how much time it took or how much it cost Him. He just loved me and wanted me home with Him. When He found me, it meant He had to clean me up, but He did.

He loves each person who ever has lived, is living now, and who will ever live. He is prepared to search like crazy to bring each one of us home where we belong— with Him. If you perk your ears up right now, you might even hear Him hanging his head out the window and hollering your name.

Scripture To Study: Luke 15:11-32
Key Verse: "…Filled with compassion, he ran to his son, embraced him, and kissed him."
Prayer: *Heavenly Father, thank You for loving me enough to chase after me… even when I sometimes run away. Thanks for cleaning me up and continuing to treat me with such amazing love. I love being in Your family! I love You, and…*

DAY 18
SHAVE YOUR EYEBROWS

My college roommate, Mike, was about to shave his eyebrows off. You would have to have known him. He would only take dares he thought no one else would. One day, he thought that shaving his eyebrows completely off would garner him some attention and be fun.

I believed in Mike's theory. Not enough to practice it myself, but enough to cheer on his craziness. So, I egged him on. "Do it, dude! Do it! No one else on campus would do this. Go for it, man!"

Mike started with the clippers on the longest setting. Bzzzzzzzzz... About the time Mike was about to move down to no guard at all, another friend of ours walked in the room. Lee lived down the hall from us and was a good friend to both of us.

I said, "Mike's gonna shave off his eyebrows! Isn't that great?"

Lee was like, "What?! Don't do it. That's a bad idea." He began to spell out why that wasn't the brightest idea and how it could impact Mike. On that night, he was a real friend to Mike, unlike me.

Proverbs 17:17 tells us, "A friend is always loyal, and a brother is born to help in time of need." I wasn't that kind of friend to Mike that night. I claimed that I loved him like a brother. That night I didn't prove it, but Lee did. Lee was the kind of friend we should all be. He stepped in and spoke up. That's the heart of God. And that's the kind of friends we should be to those around us.

How about you? Have you checked your friendship meter lately? It's never too late to begin being a terrific friend. Just walk down the hall of your life, find someone you care about, step in and speak up. They'll be glad you did, and you'll have a real friend.

Scripture To Study: Proverbs 17
Key Verse: "A friend is always loyal…"
Prayer: *Lord, I appreciate the friends You have placed in my life. Please help me to be the absolute best friend that I can possibly be toward them. Help me to be loyal and loving, to step in and speak up in their best interest… like You always do for me. I love You, and…*

DAY 19
OPTIONS

It was sometime between 2:00-3:00pm on Saturday, July 8, 1995. The temperature was over 100 degrees outside on that hot, southern afternoon as a couple hundred people gathered in the North Hodge Assembly of God church to hear PR31 and me say to each other, "I do"... and to eat the free cake at the reception.

The message by the minister, Angela's dad, mentioned something about "entering into this marriage of our own free will." We did. No one twisted our arms. That day we made a choice which limited our options for companionship "till death do us part." I am personally glad I made that choice and restricted my future options.

We were watching *Bringing Up Bates* on TV recently when Papa Bill made the following profound statement which is illustrated in the account above..."Every decision you make today determines the decisions that are available to you tomorrow."

That gives your decisions a little more weight, huh? If we make good, godly decisions today, the options available to us tomorrow should be good ones which will keep us in the will and plan of God. If, on the other hand, we make less than wise decisions today, we may be cutting ourselves out of some great opportunities for the future.

What kind of decisions are you making today?

Start now. Make the choice right now to get wisdom from God and make quality decisions according to that wisdom going forward. This one choice will set you on a trajectory toward having great future options. And don't forget, choosing not to choose is actually choosing.

Scripture To Study: James 1:5-8
Key Verse: "If you need wisdom, ask our generous God, and He will give it to you."
Prayer: *Dear Lord, I need wisdom today to make great, quality decisions which will set me up to have better options for the future. I know that You know everything and want the very best for me. Please help me in all my decision making to honor You. I love You, and...*

DAY 20
DEAR YOUNGER ME...

In Disney's movie *The Kid,* starring Bruce Willis, Willis' childhood self shows up in his adult life and causes him to face some issues from his past with which he had never dealt.

If I could go back in time, I'd tell my younger self some important info, too. Things like... "Don't eat pizza and drink Dr. Pepper till you throw up just because it tastes so good," and, "No, seriously, cut your hair". Those are fun, but there are some serious life lessons I would also teach myself:

- ***Don't be as afraid.*** Most of the stuff you're scared of is never going to happen. Almost every fear is learned, and can be unlearned. So go after life courageously!

- ***Believe God for greater.*** We think too small, dream too small, ask too small. Go big for God. Try big stuff for Him, and believe for Him to come through for you in a bigger way!

- ***Focus more on God's grace than your own performance.*** Accept that Jesus paid for all your sins and mistakes. Let His grace motivate you to live right in order to honor Him.

- ***Care less about what others think, and just be yourself.*** Forget trying to fit into other's idea of what's cool, and create your own brand. People will see you as confident and want to be like you.

- ***Try more things.*** Go after more opportunities. Learn to bake, play instruments, try out for plays, rebuild an engine of any kind, start a business before graduating high school, go on missions trips. Just keep building the list of things to try, and never stop.

We can't undo what's been done, but we can make the most of the days ahead of us. So let's go for it! That way, an older version of ourself won't have to say we should have listened to the author of that devotional book we read.

Scripture To Study: Ephesians 5:15-20
Key Verse: "Don't act thoughtlessly, but understand what the Lord wants you to do."
Prayer: *Heavenly Father, please give me insights today from my past which can help me live the way in which You would have me live. I want to live the full, abundant life which You desire for me to have. I love You, and...*

DAY 21
CRAZY WEEK

You know, it was just your average "Are you kidding me" kind of week. Teeth cleanings for the whole family led to PR31 having an unexpected dental surgery. That led to me substitute-leading the kids ministry class at our church on short notice when the kids pastor got really sick. Which led to a whopper of a 2-day garage sale run by me and our 8-year old one of the days because of the aforementioned dental surgery. Yeah, I would say was a week of the unexpected.

Transparently, some of the unexpected things that happened were amazing, and some were quite honestly, challenging. Nothing was horrific. Nothing was completely overwhelming. It was just that so much of the week was, well.. unexpected. Ever been there?

Fortunately, God knows the end from the beginning. He is never caught off-guard. He was right there with us every step of the way, working out details so that everything worked. He blessed us with success and favor, and even a lower-than-expected dental bill. So, it's not that all the unexpected stuff was negative. Someone even unexpectedly came and bought the remaining items at our garage sale, then hauled it off so that I didn't have to.

I love that we have a Heavenly Father who can handle what is unexpected to us because it's not to Him. There is nothing outside His scope. Nothing outside His perspective. Nothing that surprises Him. No lost job. No doctor's report. Nothing. That gives me a great sense of peace. It should you, too.

Honestly, I'm kind of hoping for a mundane week next week. You know, one of those boring, nothing-to-blog-about weeks. But if it's not, I know we will be just fine as long as we stick with the God, for Whom all of our breaking stories are simply old news.

Scripture To Study: Isaiah 46:1-13
Key Verse: "Only I can tell you the future before it even happens."
Prayer: *Lord, I don't know what kind of week I will face next week, but I'm glad to know that You have already seen next week, and You have everything lined up for me to survive it and succeed in it. I trust You with my life. I love You, and…*

DAY 22
UN-DRAFTED

As a kid, I was always small for my age. So, when it came to sports, I was also typically picked last. It feels pretty bad to be standing there as two people pick who they want on their team, and just hoping that you won't be the very last one chosen. It feels even worse when they have picked everyone except you, and one team leader says to the other, "You can have him." Yeah, been there, done that. So, I suppose I've always had a heart for the underdogs in life. I know what it's like to be picked last, and even not selected at all.

With my history of not really getting picked, the NFL Draft is always intriguing to me. Plenty of first-round draft picks never pan out. Some players who were drafted in later rounds who turned out to be superstars. Other players come into the NFL as un-drafted free agents. In other words, no one was willing to take a chance on them by drafting them, but later hired them. Some of these guys have turned out to be superstars.

Interestingly, Jesus picked twelve un-drafted free agents Himself. Some Biblical scholars believe the disciples were all in their teens and twenties. Most rabbis of that time chose the boys they would train to be leaders in the Jewish religion by the time they were 12 or 13 years of age. So if you didn't get "drafted" by a great rabbi, you simply went on back to pursue your family's business. That means the guys Jesus picked were almost certainly passed up by other rabbis, but that didn't stop Jesus from choosing them.

For the record, Jesus still signs un-drafted free agents today. You may have been passed up by a lot of people for a lot of things. Rest assured, God sees value in you. God sees talent and ability in you. Sign with Him, and He will show them what He can do with you!

Scripture To Study: Matthew 4:18-22
Key Verse: "They immediately followed Him, leaving the boat and their father behind."
Prayer: *Heavenly Father, I may not appear to be much to some people in this world, but I am so glad that my significance comes from the fact that You have valued me highly and paid an enormous price to bring me into Your family. Thank You! I love You, and…*

DAY 23
HE WILL MAKE YOU

Some people make music. Some people make spectacular food. Some people make art. Some people make inventions which solve problems for millions of people. I usually just make friends.

Creating doesn't usually seem to be my forte. I don't make a fuss, but I do try to make a difference. I'm not necessarily artistic. I'm not necessarily musical. I do make sermons, with the Lord's help.

Isn't that the key— the Lord's help? In Matthew 4:19, Jesus called men to follow Him as their guide and teacher. His promise to them was that He would "make them..." He would take those who were used to catching fish to feed their bellies, and He would make them into those who catch men for God's Kingdom.

The focus is on transforming them, on making them. And here's what Jesus made them:

- **Capable**— Jesus transformed them into those who had the ability to serve Him and welcome people into His family.

- **Confident**— Jesus transformed them into those who were able to stand before crowds and leaders without struggling, stammering or quivering.

- **Courageous**— Jesus transformed them into those who could stare threats, punishment and even death in the face boldly.

The Good News for us is that Jesus is the same yesterday, today and forever! The One who made them capable, confident and courageous will make you those things as well. All He asks is that you follow Him. All He asks is that you make Him your teacher, your guide, your leader, your rescuer from sin. When you make Him these things, He makes you those things!

Scripture To Study: Matthew 4:18-22
Key Verse: "Come, follow Me, and I will make you fishers of men."
Prayer: *Heavenly Father, on my own I lack what I need to be and do all that You have planned for me to be and do. But I surrender every area of my life to You completely today. And I ask You to make me into all I need to be to bring honor to You. I love You, and...*

DAY 24
SMALL AND SIGNIFICANT

Most mornings, I wake up before the rest of the family, but there are occasions when I've gotten in late or had rough night's sleep that I sleep in, and they all get going before me. Often on mornings like that, I shuffle into the kitchen to make some strong coffee only to find PR31 has already made it for me. Ahhh... It's the little things in life.

Small acts of kindness have amazing value. Small yellow sticky notes of appreciation make a big impact. People who don't feel they can accomplish much in life can have massive influence through the small touches of care and concern for those around them every day.

The old adage says, "Dynamite comes in small packages." True. So do engagement rings. So do kids who grow up to president. A lot of big things look small at first glance. Look again.

Some people have a tendency to look at others as "small," and think they lack value or don't match up, but it is a mistake to believe that size indicates impact or influence. Sometimes, it is a small group of people who make a huge difference. For example, the men who signed the Declaration of Independence. Sometimes a batch of homemade goodies from a neighbor brightens our day.

Jesus had a knack for noticing those whom others might have labeled as insignificant, and then showing just how impactful they really were. Once, He saw a widowed woman giving her last two small coins to help others and said her offering was more significant than those who had given a great deal more money.

May we be those who check our attitudes about who and what is perceived as small to make sure we do not count them as insignificant. And may we never underestimate our own ability in some "small" way to make an incredibly big difference.

Scripture To Study: Luke 21:1-4
Key Verse: "...she, poor as she is, has given everything she has."

Prayer: *Lord, I don't want to base my significance on a comparison to others. I want to honor You with my life by doing all that I can, every chance I get. Please help me to do the little things in life for others in a big way. I love You, and...*

DAY 25
TRUST UNDER ANESTHESIA

We simply went to get our family's teeth cleaned, only to find out that Angela needed oral surgery. As the oral surgeon was finishing up, Angela saw him pulling the "cat-gut" up and out of her mouth, and from her vantage point, it looked like the he was stitching up the roof of her mouth. She couldn't wait to run her tongue across the roof of her mouth to feel how far he had to stitch.

He finished his suturing, sat her up and let her know that everything was fine. Once she could manage it without being obvious, she lightly ran her tongue over the roof of her mouth, but to her surprise, there were no stitches there. It was all a matter of perspective. From where she sat, it appeared to her the surgeon was doing something which he wasn't doing at all. In the end, she simply had to trust that he knew what he was doing better than she did.

We all go through difficult situations in life... situations God allows for some reason. While He is working on us, it can appear to us He is working on something unrelated, or that He isn't working at all.

It's in those moments we need to trust God as the ultimate spiritual Surgeon. His job is to do what He does, even if it doesn't look right to us. Our job is to sit back, relax and let Him work. In the end, we'll see that His work was as perfect as He is.

I don't know what brought you to His office and set you in His chair today, but I can tell you that I've been to Him before. He's gentle. He won't hurt you. And in the end you'll be glad you let Him work on your life, regardless of what His suturing looks like while you're under the anesthesia. Just trust Him.

Scripture To Study: Romans 8:26-30
Key Verse: "And we know that God causes everything to work together for the good..."
Prayer: *Heavenly Father, I'm glad You are in control of everything in my life and that You know how to make all those things work out for my good as Your child. Today, I choose to ignore what things look like from my perspective and simply trust You. You've got this! You've got me. I love You, and...*

DAY 26
WE'RE ALL FIXER UPPERS

I am an avid fan of the hit TV show *Fixer Upper* featuring Chip and JoAnna Gaines. Part of my fascination has to do with the potential they see in the houses they fix up. The tagline in the opening theme of the show each week says, "We find the worst house in the best neighborhood and turn it into our clients' dream home." I love that! It's all about finding something that has potential, but has simply been left outdated and deteriorated.

Those reveal segments are always spectacular. Clients can't believe their eyes. As they tour the run-down house they bought which has been turned into the home of their dreams, the Gaines' explain what they did and why they did it. They show how they had to tear out and replace to make the person's home express all it's hidden potential.

The ooh's and ahh's from the clients are always worth every effort made to get the job done. From jaw drops to tears of joy, to the sheer inability to speak, to jumping up and down, the clients who trusted the Gaines' expertise reveal just how great they did on the clients' "fixer upper."

I, too, am a fixer upper whom God saw as having potential, but needing some work. He saw what needed to be demolished in my life, and what the finished design might look like. When He's done with me, the way I think, talk and behave will be so much better than before, and one day He'll reveal me as one of His finished projects.

For the record, as He surveys the neighborhood, He sees you, too, with all your potential. This is no DIY job. If you will trust Him, God will guide the process, and in the end you will be more amazing than you ever dreamed possible.

Scripture To Study: Philippians 1:3-11
Key Verse: "... He who began a good work in you will bring it to completion..."
Prayer: *Father, I am such a mess sometimes. Thank You for believing there is more to me than meets the eye. If it has to get uglier before it gets prettier in my life, please help me to be patient and trust that You will make me amazing. I love You, and...*

DAY 27
YOUR SEASON TO BLOOM

Our winter was unseasonably warm this past year. January and February usually bring some pretty brisk temperatures for those of us who are Southerners. So, it was odd to see the azalea bushes in our yard in full bloom so early in the year. Usually, these beauties don't bloom until March or April. Yet there they are, arrayed in all their glory, bees and butterflies buzzing around them, gathering nectar.

There's a part of me that wants to shout, "What are you doing?! It's not your season to bloom!" Then I sit back and laugh at myself. Who am I to tell them when to bloom? Did I create those bushes? No, I didn't even plant them. Do I understand how they gather nutrients... or process light energy using photosynthesis... or create pollen which bees use to make honey... or absorb carbon dioxide that I breathe out in order to produce the oxygen that I breathe in? No. No, I do not.

I'm like Job in the Bible, who was trying to explain to God that it wasn't right he was having to go through all the problems he faced. When God asked Job where he was when He began to create the world out of nothing, Job understood that he was out of his pay grade.

Perhaps you are doing something great, and God is opening doors for you to walk through that you can't explain to others. Maybe people in your life look at what you are attempting, and say to you, "What are you doing? It's not your season to bloom."

When it's your time to bloom, bloom. God determines our seasons. He doesn't wait to check and see if it would be okay with others if we go ahead and bloom. He just changes the atmosphere and lets the buds turn into blossoms. So, if He's okay with you blooming, it really doesn't matter what others think about it. Just bloom.

Scripture To Study: Job 38:1 - 40:5
Key Verse: "I have said too much already."
Prayer: *Heavenly Father, if You say it's my time to bloom in life, then set the atmosphere and make it conducive to my blooming. I am ready to bloom whenever and however You determine is best. Just let me bloom beautifully and point people to you. I love You, and...*

DAY 28
DO IT ANYWAY

Is there something people have told you would be impossible for you? Is there something they say you don't have the skills, or talent, or education, or finances to accomplish? You're not the only one who has ever experienced this. David in the Old Testament was the shepherd boy who became the king of his nation. All through his life, he had people telling him that he could not accomplish great things:

- When the prophet Samuel came to David's home to anoint the next king of Israel, David's dad called all of his sons to be presented to the prophet... except David. Yet David was chosen and became king.

- When his dad sent him to check on his brothers during a battle, only to discover Goliath taunting God's people, David's brother told him, "You have no business fighting in this battle." But David did fight, and became the champion of the Israelites that very day.

- King Saul said David would never be king of Israel, chased him like a fugitive, and proclaimed that David could not escape the manhunt, but David escaped many times on his way to becoming king.

- When David became king over all Israel, the people of Jebus told David he would never conquer their city. But David did conquer their city, and it became known as "The City of David."

Maybe someone has told you that you would never amount to much in life. That you can't live debt-free. That you could never earn that degree. That you can't start that business. Or speak publicly. Or get married. Or be a great parent. *Do it anyway!*

If God says you can, you can. If you are willing and obedient to God, then nothing can stop you. Go ahead and do it anyway!

Scripture To Study: II Samuel 5:6-10
Key Verse: "...he called it the City of David..."
Prayer: *Lord, there are plenty of people who can tell me that I can't do something great for You, but all it takes is for You to say that I can, and I will. I want to accomplish all that I can for You during my lifetime. Please help me do it despite the naysayers. I love You, and...*

DAY 29
UNEXPECTED PUMPKINS

We carved pumpkins with the boys this past October. It's an annual tradition. We don't do scary, but we definitely do fun. And the boys— including me— have fun carving pumpkins.

We sat on the grass near the entryway of our house, and we carved pumpkins. I cut the top openings to reveal the inner goop. The boys scooped out all the goop and seeds to clean out the pumpkins so we could carve our designs and put tea-light candles down inside them.

We tried to get most of the goop and seeds into an old plastic shopping sack, but of course, we missed some seeds. Usually, the birds take care of anything we leave behind. So, we didn't worry about it.

I had not thought about those carved pumpkins since we threw away their molded, rotting remains some time in late November... that is until yesterday. I came home to all kinds of fun PR31 and the boys had cooked up. One surprise was two pumpkin plants growing in our yard.

I had no idea we were planting pumpkins last fall. We didn't think we had planted any seeds. We probably thought we picked them all up, but we certainly planted some pumpkin seeds. Now they are producing plants which could possibly produce more pumpkins.

The same is true in each of our lives. We are each planting seeds of whatever we are, wherever we go. Paul told the folks in the church at Galatia, "You will always harvest what you plant." Sometimes, we don't even realize we are planting.

This is why it is crucial that we make sure our life is full of goodness and godliness. Because what we plant is *always* going to be what we harvest... whether we know we planted it or not. I suspect there will be some unexpected harvests for each of us in eternity. That should motivate us to plant good stuff at every turn.

Scripture To Study: Galatians 6:1-10
Key Verse: "... You will always harvest what you plant."
Prayer: *Father, You have established the principle of harvesting what we plant. I want to plant good things. Please help me to plant only good words and actions so that I harvest only good in return. Thanks! I love You, and...*

DAY 30
CELEBRATE THOSE IN THE SHADOWS

Some people get stage fright. Not me. I get stage delight. Put me on a platform, put a microphone in my hand, and cut me loose. It is very often my happy place. It's not that the stage fills an emotional void in my life. It's just part of how God designed me. Whether it is preaching, presenting or performing, I enjoy being in front of a group of people.

But I am also acutely aware I would never be able to stand on a stage comfortably or excel at what I'm doing there without those "hidden figures" who do what they do offstage, behind the scenes, where possibly no one will ever know that they did what they did.

I like to celebrate those people. Too many times I have been the person to get the pat on the back because I was on the platform, but I know all too well that I didn't turn on the lights. Or clean the restrooms. Or write the script. Or feed the hungry. Or hug an orphan. Or write the code. Or build the set. Or empty a bedpan. There are people doing acts of service quietly, where no one notices.

Scripture tells us in Romans 13:7 to give "honor to whom honor is due." People behind the scenes deserve to be honored and recognized for all their service.

Who is it in your life that is "behind the scenes" making your life better? Why not take time today to look them in the eyes, smile at them, and tell them, "Thanks!" Or if you can't meet them in person, jot them a note of thanks. Or post a pic of them doing their job on social media, and give them a public shout-out of appreciation.

Scripture To Study: Romans 13:1-10
Key Verse: "Pay… respect to whom respect is owed, honor to whom honor is owed."
Prayer: *Dear Lord, You have blessed my life with so many people who help me in so many ways. I am grateful for them. Please help me to express my appreciation to as many as possible today, and to continue expressing that appreciation throughout life. I love You, and…*

THE UPSIDE

DAY 31
ONE CHAPTER AT A TIME

I have begun the life of an author. I think one of the greatest surprises in writing has been that, even though I know what a book is about, have a general idea of where I'm headed with it, have chapter titles, and may have completed the rough draft on some of it, I don't know exactly how each of the following chapters will come about. It is actually very much like reading a book. You know the title. You know what you've read so far. You know what you think might be coming. But you don't really know exactly what to expect.

Scripture points out that God has recorded in a book each day of each one of our lives. In other words, our lives have chapters... chapters we have already read, and some yet to be read. Unlike me, though, God finished the book on each of our lives before a single day had passed.

Think about that for a moment. He wrote down every day before a single one took place. That means He knows what is coming, even though we are just following along chapter-by-chapter. He is never caught off-guard. He is never surprised. He is never shocked.

We, on the other hand, can think that we know where the Author is headed with our lives, but we don't know all the exact twists and turns of the plot. Our world often gets upended with one phone call. With one doctor's report. With one grade. With one job interview. Sometimes those newfound experiences are glorious. Sometimes they are grueling.

The good news is that God turns the pages for us at just the right pace. So, even if we don't know what's coming... He does. And He knows how everything will turn out. So, hang in there. There are great chapters coming... if you stick with the author.

Scripture To Study: Psalm 139
Key Verse: "...Every day of my life was recorded in Your book..."
Prayer: *Dear Lord, it amazes me how detailed Your plan is for my life. I realize I don't always see how that plan is going to come together, but I trust You. Please help me to follow You through the chapters of this life. I love You, and...*

DAY 32
THAT PHONE CALL

Austin woke up before Alex yesterday morning. So, I took time to read to him from their VeggieTales devotional. The devotion was about letting God help you have the self-control to be patient in order to make the wisest decision. We finished reading, prayed together, and went about our day.

I was beginning to feel pressured about a decision we needed to make and which we had been researching for a couple of months. So, I asked the Lord to help me have patience to make the best decision.

Later that day, we came to a point of decision. I talked it over with Angela, and we agreed that we were making a solid decision. As we wrapped up our talk, I felt compelled that we should pray. We stopped, and prayed a really short prayer for God to give us wisdom.

We sought advice one more time, but there was this slight hesitation. During this hesitation, my phone rang. I sent it to voicemail, but at the end of the discussion decided to return the call.

That interrupting call offered me a different option with a better result. We suddenly had peace in our hearts and knew this new choice was the way to go. In the end, we saved over $1,000.

Psalm 37:23 says that God delights in every detail of our lives. He finds joy in helping us with everything we're facing in life. No matter how big or how small the details of your life, God cares. He takes notice. He's interested, and He will get involved to your benefit if you'll just invite Him to do so.

Your prayer doesn't have to be big or fancy. Just open your life to His involvement. Why not go ahead and stop right now to ask God to get involved in every detail of your life? He's waiting for you to ask. He wants to help. Go ahead... I'll stop writing now so the two of you can talk.

Scripture To Study: Psalm 37
Key Verse: "The Lord directs the steps of the godly…"
Prayer: *Father, thank You for helping me make right decisions and avoid wrong ones. I need You more than I can say. I'm sure I need You more than I know. Please guide me today. I love You, and…*

DAY 33
BE LIKE FINGERNAILS

During my first of two years playing little league baseball, our coach was teaching us to bunt. I must have missed something when he showed us how to hold the bat because, when it was my turn to practice, I turned my body and held the bat between my chest and waist. When the pitch came, it smashed my middle finger between the ball and the bat. The collision of ball with finger resulted in splitting my fingernail in two and producing a significant amount of blood. Coach tried to stop the bleeding until Mom and Dad arrived to pick me up from practice. Then they properly bandaged it at home.

When I was finally allowed to take the bandage off a week later, something odd happened. One part of the split nail just fell off. A couple days, the other part fell off, leaving me with a nailless finger. It was a weird, tender sensation. I really had to protect it for awhile to keep from reopening the wound.

I learned something important over the following weeks... fingernails keep growing. After healing up, it began to push new fingernail growth from under the cuticle and eventually returned to full length. That nail still has a ridge down the middle of it where it split, but it grows like all the rest of my fingernails.

I want to be like a fingernail. I want to keep growing. I may get bitten, cut or even smashed in life, but I want to keep growing. Scripture tells us in Jeremiah 17:8 that we can be like trees planted by a riverbank and have roots which run down deep into the water. It goes on to say that trees like this just keeping on producing fruit all the time.

Never let anyone underestimate who you are and what you are capable of. Fingernails are useful little things. So, my call today is to be like fingernails... keep on growing regardless of what happens to you.

Scripture To Study: Jeremiah 17:1-10
Key Verse: "...they never stop producing fruit."
Prayer: *Lord, thank You for being my source. With You, I know that I can keep growing and accomplishing all you have designed me to produce. Please help me to keep growing. I love You, and...*

DAY 34
CAN'T HEAR GOD?

For those of us who were alive and old enough to understand what happened, the terrorist attacks on our country on September 11, 2001 will never be forgotten. And as bad as that time in our country was, one moment really stood out and inspired me during that time.

It was the day President George W. Bush visited New York City to view the damage and encourage the workers who were still cleaning up rubble and looking for survivors. He stood on a makeshift platform with megaphone in hand and began speaking to the crowd of tired workers. Then someone in the crowd interrupted his speech by hollering out, "We can't hear you!" To which he immediately responded— off the cuff— "That's okay... You may not be able to hear me, but I can hear you. The whole world can hear you. And soon the people who did this are going to hear all of us!" It was an inspiring, soul-lifting, patriotic moment. The crowd cheered. We all cheered.

We all cheered that day because it's great to know that you've been heard. Sometimes, it's easy to feel like we can't hear God. And it's even easier to feel like— if you can't hear Him— maybe He can't hear you. But like President Bush said to that tired worker, feeling unheard that day because he couldn't hear the President speak, God says to us, "I can hear you!"

Scripture time and again tells us that God is the God who listens and hears. He turns His ear toward us, even bending low to hear every word we utter.

There is not a prayer you've prayed which hasn't been heard. God is listening intently, and even though you may feel like He hasn't heard you, He definitely has. And He is working on your behalf to make sure that your request is answered in the right way. At the right time. For your benefit. God hears you. Don't give up.

Scripture To Study: Psalm 17
Key Verse: "...I know you will answer..."
Prayer: *Heavenly Father, I love that You listen to me. Thank You for hearing my prayers, and answering. Please help me to always remember that you hear me and will answer. I love You, and...*

DAY 35
A BROWN'S LANDING LIFE

Pappaw took me and the boys on a guys-only fishing trip, and it was pretty cool outside that morning. Somehow, I failed to pack appropriate shoes for the boys because it was warm when we left our house, and so they were wearing flip-flops. It was too cold to fish in flip-flops that day. Alex opted to wear his house-shoes, which inspired us to pick up some clearance house-shoes for Austin.

When we got close to the lake, Pappaw mentioned that we needed to go into the store at Brown's Landing, the store at the boat launch which sells snacks, beverages, bait, tackle and fuel. As we pulled into the parking area and pulled to a stop, Austin asked if we were going inside the store. Pappaw said we were and asked why.

Austin inquired if he and Alex would be allowed inside since they were only wearing house-shoes. I love Pappaw's reply... "Of course, you can. Brown's isn't a fancy place. You can just go in there like you are." This pleased Austin immensely because he wanted to go inside, but didn't know if he could because of his shoes.

Jesus said in the Gospels that it is the sick who need a doctor. In other words, God's people should be willing to accept people as they are in order for God to do His work in them.

Oh, that someone like Pappaw could say to those in need around me, "Of course, you can... That's Allen... He isn't fancy... You can be a friend of his just like you are... I've seen him accept people in worse condition than you into his life. When you get in his life, you'll meet the God who has what you need."

Could someone introduce you that way? Or do you have a "no shirt, no shoes, no service" policy in your life? C'mon, let's live like Brown's Landing!

Scripture To Study: Mark 2:13-17
Key Verse: "(There were many people of this kind among Jesus' followers.)"
Prayer: *Dear Lord, thank You for never turning me away. Please help me to have that same attitude toward those You love so much who don't know You yet. I love You, and...*

DAY 36
HARVEST OR LOST SEED?

I love a painting I saw in Israel which depicts farmers sadly planting crops in all these deep reds and oranges, then harvesting in all bright yellows and greens. In between, is a portion that is blue. It is based on Psalm 126:5-6, which reads, "*Those who plant in tears will harvest with shouts of joy. They weep as they go to plant their seed, but they sing as they return with the harvest.*"

In the time of that Psalm's writing, most people were farmers, and when they harvested crops, they set aside some of the seeds to plant the next year. The problem was, success was not guaranteed. Success depended on the right amounts of rain and sunshine.

Every handful of seed they planted was a handful of grain they couldn't use to feed themselves or their family right then, but if they used the grain to feed themselves right then, there would certainly be no food for the future. So they planted with tears because it was a tough decision. Plus, its result wouldn't be seen for months.

The amount they planted was based on how much faith they had and how much they were willing to sacrifice at the moment. The more faith they used, the more it took to leave that seed in the ground and wait. Yet, if they trusted the Lord, He blessed their planting, and they harvested in joy!

We, too, decide whether or not we will invest in the lives of others here and now in hopes of what *might* be harvested later. It's a decision of faith. Will I love, encourage and give to people now in hopes there will be love, encouragement and generosity for me later?

How much we plant in the lives of others is still based on faith. The level at which we plant determines the level at which we will harvest. So, if you happen to pass me and see me weeping, don't worry too much. I'm just planting in faith, and there will be a harvest. I can count on it. And so can you!

Scripture To Study: Psalm 126
Key Verse: "... plant in tears... harvest with shouts of joy."
Prayer: *Father, thank You for giving me the ability to plant love and encouragement into the lives of others. Please help me plant in faith, believing I will have enough later. I love You, and…*

THE UPSIDE

DAY 37
LIFE WITHOUT TRAINING WHEELS

Our youngest son, Austin, began riding his bike without training wheels recently. He probably could have done it before now, but he wasn't ready. We tried once, and he decided that he preferred to have them on a little longer.

Then one day, with trepidation and maybe a little extra coaxing from me, he decided he would attempt it again. He rode across the driveway a few times with me jogging along behind and holding the bike steady by the seat. I would occasionally let go. He did fine, but he still wasn't sure he was ready. Yet, I did not put the training wheels back on this time.

The next day, the boys were outside playing, and I walked out to find Austin riding his bike without training wheels pretty well. Alex had coached him, and he was making great progress. The more he rode, the better he got. He soon discovered the training wheels, while helpful, were actually holding him back and slowing him down.

The truth is, God has new seasons for us in which we will no longer need those training wheels. He has something wonderful for us, and those "training wheels" are only slowing us down.

Solomon pointed out in Ecclesiastes 3:1 that there are seasons for everything in our lives. There are new seasons for new excitement and new enjoyment. Times of going slower and times of going faster.

It's time to let God take off those "training wheels" which have given you security up to this point in life. It won't be long until you are out there riding at full speed while He watches in sheer joy as His child enjoys newfound excitement, adventure and possibilities. Shake off those nerves... trust your Heavenly Father... and ride like the wind!

Scripture To Study: Ecclesiastes 3:1-8
Key Verse: "For everything, there is a season, a time for every activity under Heaven."
Prayer: *Lord, thank You for preparing new seasons of life for me. Please stay beside me as I launch into these new endeavors. Sometimes I don't feel too stable on my own. I need You with me so that I can feel secure till I am comfortable with it all. I love You, and...*

DAY 38
PERSISTENCE PAYS OFF

Yeah, our dog is spoiled. We know it. It's a fact that can be documented if necessary. The truth is, she fits in great with our family. Every last one of us is spoiled. PR31 is the baby in her family, as am I in mine. Since we weren't able to have kids for so long, when God finally blessed us with them, we have perhaps gone a little beyond what is required in life in providing for them from time to time.

So, it's no surprise to me that Sugar the Schnauzer would be spoiled. She has plenty of examples to follow. This morning I was eating an apple, and she came begging at my recliner. I told her "No" at first— very firmly, mind you— but she didn't stop sitting there patiently, looking up at me with those longing eyes.

I caved. I gave in, and gave her one small bite off of one slice of apple. "Now that's all," I proclaimed. But she kept sitting... and staring longingly... and waiting... hoping for more apple. So, I gave her another piece. Why drag this out? You probably know I ended up giving her another piece or two after that as she continued to do everything but ask me politely in so many words.

I suppose I should be more like Sugar. I should follow the Lord wherever He goes, sit down in front of Him, look longingly at Him, and wait for Him to bless me. I mean, I am well-schooled in the art of being a spoiled kid. Plus, I know how I love to bless our sons. Why then do I give up so easily when I don't see a prayer answered on day one? Why do I quit when the Lord says, "No," at first? Sometimes I probably miss out on what God has for me simply because I give up too soon.

Our loving God hears us and responds to us as we persist with Him. We're not bothering Him. We're believing Him for those good things we believe He is willing to give us or do for us in life. And now, if you'll please excuse me... I need to go ask again. Don't you?

Scripture To Study: Luke 18:1-8
Key Verse: "...they should always pray and never give up."
Prayer: *Heavenly Father, thank You for being so generous to me. Thank You for not getting upset when I continue to ask You to bless me. Please help me to not give up too easily when You are more than willing to help me. I love You, and...*

DAY 39
THE SAME, BUT DIFFERENT

The boys recently discovered Super Mario Brothers for Nintendo Wii. It's fun watching a new generation enjoy the game. It brings back memories for both me and Angela. We actually still own the original NES (Nintendo Entertainment System), and we pull it out on rare occasions to relive "the glory days." We also have a blast learning the new twists and turns of the Wii version. Though there are a few new characters, a few new tools and a few new play areas, the goal is still the same... rescue Princess Peach. Characters still basically operate the same, and you still move left to right on the screen.

It hit me yesterday that our goal for believers is still the same today as it was 20 years ago, 200 years ago, even 2,000 years ago. The mission and message are still the same today. Only some of the methods are new.

Just like the boys use a different machine, the graphics are a lot clearer and the controller is more responsive yet they are still playing the same basic game, so we as believers today have some pretty sweet new ways to present the same great message, the same Good News... Jesus came to pay the price for everyone's crimes against God so that we could go free and become a part of God's family forever!

We may use social media or movies to convey the Good News instead of standing on the street corner preaching or holding a massive crusade under a tent, but the truth remains the same. Jesus still transforms us from sinners to saints. I love that Jesus is the same yesterday, today and forever (Hebrews 13:8). And whether you're old school or new school, those of us who love Jesus are all on the same mission. Share Him with others!

Now I have to quit typing and give my thumbs a rest... gotta save up some skills to show those boys a thing or two!

Scripture To Study: Matthew 28:16-20
Key Verse: "Therefore, go and make disciples of all the nations..."
Prayer: *Dear Lord, thank You for giving me the privilege of sharing Your love with others. Please help me to find creative new ways to present You to people in a positive way today. I love You, and...*

DAY 40
LOVE THEM ANYWAY

It's Scrooge in Charles Dickens' A Christmas Carol. It's the person at school, or on the job, or across the street. There are people who are just difficult to love. Sometimes they are jerks. Sometimes they are rude. Whatever the case, they have their defenses up.

Love them anyway. Bake them cookies. Mow their grass for them. Take up the slack at work on a project with which they are struggling.

Or my personal favorite... Hug them. I like to give them a strong and long hug. I like for it to be awkward for them. It's okay. I'm a hugger. It's awkward for lots of folks, but when they need to be loved and act like they don't want to, it's the best.

They just can't decide whether to push you away or hug you back even tighter. Usually they push you away first. That's okay. Keep hugging them. At some point, they'll break. When they do, get ready because you are about to be hugged back like never before.

Not sure you can do this? Well, it's what Jesus does for every one of us until we finally accept His love. His forgiveness. His grace. His life-transforming power. He just loves us anyway.

We act like jerks to Him, He hugs us. We push Him away by doing things we know He doesn't like or approve of, He hugs us. He just loves us despite what we say or act like because He knows we need it most. He touched the lepers, those society said were off-limits, and He's been hugging people like us ever since.

So, you have someone in your life who isn't so easy to get along with? To quote my sweet friend, Jeanne Mayo, "Be Jesus with skin on." When your eyes meet theirs, plaster a big ol' smile on your face, spread your arms wide open, and wrap them up.

Give it time and lots of hugs. One day, they'll hug back, and you won't have to plaster that smile on. It will show up on its own.

Scripture To Study: Luke 5:12-16
Key Verse: "Jesus reached out and touched him..."
Prayer: *Father, thank You for loving and reaching out to me, even when I don't treat You in the right way. Please help me to reach out to others who are difficult to love in Your power. I love You, and...*

DAY 41
IN CASE...

Perhaps you think that, because this book could be in the hands of almost anyone anywhere, there is no way I know who is reading this or what is going through your mind and heart. I suppose you are partly correct, but I know what I'm writing is for someone specific... even though I don't know whom yet. Here it goes anyway...

In case no one has ever told you... I love you. I love you not because you are always good. I love you even when you know you don't match up to what is right.

In case no one has ever told you... I'm proud of you. You make me smile. You're amazing!

In case no one has ever told you... You are talented, gifted and creative in a way that no one else on earth can match or replicate. You have abilities which are off the charts.

In case no one has ever told you... You are attractive. People want to get to know you because there is something intriguing and wonderful about you.

In case no one has ever told you... You are capable of accomplishing so much good in life. You have crazy potential stored up inside you.

In case no one has ever told you... I value you more than you can possibly imagine. You are important.

How can I say those things to you? Well, I tried to put myself in God's shoes for just a moment. As I opened my heart to His, I sensed that these are the things He would say to you right now if you gave Him the opportunity to sit down and talk with you face-to-face.

What if you did? What if you just took a moment right now... read those words again... closed your eyes... and imagined God saying them to you? What if you let them sink down deep into your heart? What if you took a chance and believed He means it?

Scripture To Study: Genesis 1:1-31
Key Verse: "Then God looked over all He had made, and He saw that it was very good!
Prayer: *Sweet Father, thank You for believing in me. Please help me to see in me what You see in me like never before. I love You, and...*

DAY 42
BROKEN?

Do you feel broken? Do you feel like your heart is shattered all over the floor in little shards... some pieces so small they might never be found? Do you wonder if anyone could ever put you back together and make you valuable again?

Rest assured, God says in His Word that He heals the broken-hearted and bandages their wounds. Jesus quotes the Old Testament prophet Isaiah to describe Himself and His role as The Rescuer of mankind, and He says one element of what He does is "bind up the broken-hearted."

He proved it over and over as He walked this earth. He proved it with Zacchaeus... with the woman caught in the very act of cheating on her spouse... with a guy controlled by myriad demons... with the Samaritan woman who had been married five times and was at the time shacking-up with a different guy... with friends and family who would turn their backs on Him... with the very soldiers who nailed Him to a cross... and even with the thieves who cursed Him as He was dying.

Oh, He most certainly cares about the broken in this world. He cares enough to stop for them. He cares enough to pick up all their broken pieces, put them back together and restore them to amazing beauty and functionality.

If you are broken right now, then know this... He cars for you. You are in a good place for God to step in, heal your hurts and bandage you up. Remember, though the scars remain, the scars don't have to remind you that you've been hurt. Instead, they can remind you that you have been healed.

Scripture To Study: Isaiah 61:1-11
Key Verse: "The Spirit of the Sovereign Lord is upon me, for the Lord has appointed me to bring good news to the poor. He has sent me to comfort the brokenhearted..."

Prayer: *Lord, thank You for healing my hurts. You alone know the depth of the pain I have endured. You alone know what will take the pain away. You alone can put all the broken pieces of my heart back together perfectly. Please comfort me today. I love You, and...*

DAY 43
SCARS

Alex stood there in his PJ's looking down at his foot. He said, "Wow, Daddy! In just a couple weeks, it will be one year since I got this cut on my foot when the chair fell over on it. Look, now there is only a small scar there. It's not even really red anymore. You can barely see it." When it happened, Alex was in a lot of pain. That wound had to be bandaged and re-bandaged. It took days for the initial wound to close up, but it did close up, and continued to heal.

So it is with wounds. Some wounds take longer to heal than others, but if treated properly, they will heal up. Sometimes there are scars. Some people try to hide their scars or have them removed. Some people bear their scars as a mark of honor. They want people to know they've been wounded and survived.

Scars are reminders that there *was* once a wound. Now it is healed, or at least is healing. Some wounds are so deep and hurt so badly that, when we first incur them, we wonder if they will ever heal. Even as we bandage them, we grimace. Days go by, and the pain is still there. Weeks go by, and we remember the injury very clearly when we bump it on something.

Over time, wounds heal, and scars develop. We remember that it happened. We know it hurt. We recall the days of tenderly nursing it, but we don't feel the pain we did at the time.

And we are able to say to our Heavenly Father as we look down at our wound, "Wow, Daddy! Look, it doesn't look nearly as bad as it did then. All I see now is the healed place where the hurt once was."

For the record, Christ has scars, too. His scars show that He, too, was wounded. His wounds healed also and serve as reminders that the pain will go away. It will fade and you will be able to enjoy life again.

Scripture To Study: John 20:24-29
Key Verse: "…Put your hand into the wound in My side…"
Prayer: *Dear Lord, thank You for showing me that it is okay to have scars. The fact that You have scars, too, helps me know that I'll make it. Please help me get past these hurts and heal. I love You, and…*

DAY 44
LIMITLESS

Our life is limited. I can run, but even if I increase my speed with great diligence and practice, I am still limited. I can increase my strength, and thereby the amount of weight I can lift, but I am still limited. I can increase my finances, but at some point there is no more time in a day for me to earn more money, and I find myself limited.

We are limited beings. We can only be in one place at a time. We can only experience one time at a time. We can only achieve certain levels in any area of life because... we are limited. I can grow, learn, expand, train and do all I want, but at some point I push my limits. Others may have limits beyond mine, but they too are limited.

"Wow, Allen... thanks for that. I thought this was called *The Upside*. How is this uplifting, encouraging or inspiring?

Well, how about this? Although we are limited, God has no limits, and therefore will never come to a place where He is pushing them. He never pushes His limits... because He has none.

God is not limited by distance. Or time. Or finances. Or strength. Or knowledge. Or speed... or... well, anything. There is no way in which He is restricted or limited. I love that, when I have come to my limits, He can still go so far beyond them. When I am tapped out, He is barely getting started. Nothing is too big for Him. Nothing taxes Him. Nothing stretches Him or stresses Him. He can always out-do Himself. There is no stopping His abilities. It's mind-boggling, really.

That's great news because it means that everything which seems out of the realm of possibility for me is not for Him. When I am weak, winded and weary, He steps in and surprises me again.

Are you at the end of your money? Your health? Your friends? Your joy? Your time? How about engaging the Limitless One and inviting Him to step into your situation? Go ahead. Give Him a try. I guarantee He's not even going to break a sweat.

Scripture To Study: Luke 1:26-38
Key Verse: "For nothing is impossible with God."
Prayer: *Lord, thank You for always being more than enough. I am at the end of my rope. Please come through for me. I love You, and...*

DAY 45
GOD FLIES

I was jolted awake in the middle of the night. Alex had cried out from their bedroom across the hall, "Daddy! Daddy! Daddy!" I jumped up and went hurriedly to where he was in his bed. Before I could even get there, he had called out to me again, and I asked him what was wrong. He paused, then replied, "Oh, nothing. Never mind." And with that, as I sat beside him, he laid back down, and went immediately back to sleep.

He went back to sleep immediately. I, on the other hand, did not. That shot of pure adrenaline that flows into your system when you think there is danger or injury related to your child was being pumped through my arteries and veins with quite a surge.

So, I ended up getting up and having plenty of time to spend with the Lord... in the middle of the night... in the quiet. Those often turn out to be some of my favorite times with Him. There is something special about how still and quiet the house is at that time.

In the wee hours of that morning, I read in Psalm 18 how God flies to our rescue when we cry out to Him in distress. It was my experience with Alex that recalled to the forefront of my thinking that I had read somewhere God does that for His kids. So I searched it out in His Word, and sure enough, God does fly to our rescue.

He doesn't just amble. Or mosey. Or saunter. No, that Psalm informs us that He rushes— indeed, He mounts a mighty cherub and flies— to our rescue when we simply cry out to Him.

Of course He does. If I— a limited, finite, imperfect dad— can be roused from my snoring, then certainly my perfect Heavenly Father who never sleeps rushes to me when I cry out to Him.

He will fly to your rescue, too, when you cry out to Him. You can count on it. Go for it. Give a holler. He is already prepping for His flight!

Scripture To Study: Psalm 18
Key Verse: "Mounted on a mighty angelic being, He flew..."
Prayer: *Father, thank You for always rushing to my rescue when I cry out to You. It's good to know You're listening and ready to act. I love You, and...*

DAY 46
GOD SPEAKS

When Alex awoke in the middle of the night crying out, "Daddy, Daddy, Daddy," I mentioned yesterday that I *rushed* to his bedside to let him know I was there with him. And that is what God does when we as His children cry out to Him.

But I also spoke to Alex and let him know that I was there. If I had been silent, it might have creeped him out even worse. Or he may not have realized I was there at all because he was actually dreaming and not truly awake. So, I responded to his cries with words of comfort.

And in Psalm 18, we find that God not only flies to our rescue, but while He is on the way toward us, He responds to our cries by speaking. Scripture says His voice "resounded." That word is defined by the Merriam-Webster dictionary app this way...
- "to become filled with sound"
- "to make a loud, deep sound"
- "to make a strong impression or have a great effect on people"

This is what happened when Jesus spoke to the wind and waves when He was in the boat with the disciples during a terrible storm which threatened to take their lives. He told the storm to, "Be quiet! Be still!" He filled the storm... and the boat... and the disciples' hearts... with His voice. And did it ever make a strong impression! Did it ever have a great effect! Immediately the storm died down around them, and the disciples were amazed at His power.

So today, as you cry out to the Lord in distress, know that He will not only rush to your rescue, but He will also respond with a resounding voice on the way to calm the situation. Stop. Turn the ears of your heart and mind. Listen. He's headed your way. Calling your name. Reassuring you, and letting anything which is coming against you know that it's time is up... now!

Scripture To Study: Psalm 18
Key Verse: "...the voice of the Most High resounded..."
Prayer: *Dear Lord, please speak Your calming words to my heart and mind today. I need to hear Your voice speaking "Peace! Be Still!" to my stormy situation. I love You, and...*

DAY 47
GOD REACHES

Beginning Wednesday morning, October 14, 1987 and for the next couple of days, the nation was riveted to TV screens watching the rescue of "Baby Jessica" McClure, then 18 months old, who had fallen 22 feet into an 8-inch wide open well at her family's home. Rescuers worked 58 hours to get down to Jessica and get her out. The man who finally made it down the 30-inch parallel shaft was double-jointed in his shoulders, which allowed him to squeeze into the tight space and make the rescue possible. The rescue took a lot of people, but it was that man who reached down himself to get her and bring her back up.

Scripture says that each of us have fallen short of God's glorious standard of perfection, love, and goodness. We are all, in a sense, like Baby Jessica... fallen and trapped.

But in our distress, we can cry out to God for help. And when He hears, He rushes... He responds... and He reaches out to rescue us.

He doesn't just call out instructions to us as to how to get out on our own. He doesn't tell us why we are bad for having fallen. He doesn't tell us that it's our fault we fell. He doesn't talk about how much it's going to take to get us out. He doesn't talk about how dirty He would have to get in order to get us out.

He just reaches. Reaches out His clean hand to grab hold of our dirty hand. Reaches out His strong hand to grab hold of our weak hand. He reaches out when we are distressed by our sin for sure, but He also reaches out to us in times of financial, relational, emotional and physical distress. Regardless of your distress, God reaches your direction.

So, when you see that strong, loving, capable Hand of your Creator reaching down in your direction, reach up and grab it. He'll do the rest!

Scripture To Study: Psalm 18
Key Verse: "He reached down from Heaven and rescued me"
Prayer: *Dear Lord, thank You for spanning the gap between me and You. I need You more than I can possibly say to reach out today and pull me up to higher levels with You. I love You, and...*

DAY 48
GOD DELIGHTS

PR31 makes me smile. I love to see her caught up in cooking a meal from scratch... mixing biscuit dough with her hands... or cracking an egg for chocolate chip cookies... or seasoning a roast to put in the crock pot. I like to watch her just doing her thing. It makes me smile.

My kids make me smile, too. I love to see them conquer a new level on Super Mario Brothers. Or get a 100 on a test they thought was challenging. Or sing like no one is listening. Or fall asleep in their seat on a road trip. It just makes me smile. It delights me.

I am hard pressed to think of something that I would not do for those three. I would go to extreme lengths for them because I love them, and in that love, they delight me.

Psalm 18 says that God rushes to our rescue. He responds to us on His way to rescue us. He reaches down to rescue us when we cry out to Him in distress. Since we know that God rescues us in our distress, why does the Psalmist feel the need to say it again in verse 19?

I believe that he writes it again to show us *why* God rescues us. He doesn't have to rescue us. He doesn't owe us anything. In fact, it's quite the opposite. We owe Him everything. The only thing He could get in return is... well, us. Yet He rescues us anyway. Why?

It's simple. He delights in us. No matter who you are, or what you've done, God loves you. And when we accept adoption into His family, there is a delight we bring to His heart. A delight that drives Him to do what might seem ridiculous to others. And so He flies, responds and reaches to rescue us out of sheer delight.

So, if you are in a crisis today... if your situation seems overwhelming... if you aren't sure which way to turn... I'd like to suggest that you cry out to God today from your heart. Your cry for help will touch His heart and will make Him smile.

Scripture To Study: Psalm 18
Key Verse: "He reached down from Heaven and rescued me"
Prayer: *Father, I love that I make You smile. I'm not sure that I always deserve that smile, but I am really glad to see it there. Thanks for making me Your beloved child. I love You, and...*

DAY 49
GOD REWARDS

Drive past any stop sign in almost any subdivision in almost any suburb, and you can be certain at some point to see a homemade poster with a picture of someone's dog and a message which reads the dog is lost. Typically, there is a reward offered for anyone who will do the right thing and return the dog if they have found it. Depending on how much the family cares about the lost dog, the amount of the reward can be somewhat substantial.

What is a reward? A reward is not pay like wages. Instead, it is recognition and appreciation shown for someone who did the right thing, even when they didn't have to.

Psalm 18:20 tells us that God rewards us for doing the right thing. What right thing? Well, since this whole passage is about going through a difficult situation, it means God rewards us for keeping a right attitude when people treat us wrong. He rewards us when we keep our joy in the midst of loss. He rewards us when we are faithful and generous in our giving to the needs of others in the midst of our own financial challenges. He rewards us when we love instead of hate.

It's not always easy to do the right thing. When people are gossiping about you. When bills pile up. When your heart feels like it has been broken into a million pieces, doing the right thing is not always what springs to mind immediately. But when we choose to do the right thing, God rewards us for doing what did not come easiest.

I don't know what distressing situation you are going through right now, and I'm sure that it is possible you don't really feel like doing the right thing. But I can assure you that if you will do the next right thing right now, you'll be stronger and better able to do the next right thing after that. And in the end, God is going to reward you for doing right.

Scripture To Study: Psalm 18
Key Verse: "He reached down from Heaven and rescued me"
Prayer: *Heavenly Father, I know I don't earn Your love or forgiveness. Thank You for rewarding me when I do right after having been done wrong. And thanks, Jesus, for Your example of how to do that. I love You, and...*

DAY 50
GOD RESTORES

I have a problem. I see potential. I see a closed-down building... or a piece of old furniture sitting street-side in front of someone's house... or a dilapidated house... and I see potential. I see what used to be and also what could be. And it's a problem because I have neither the time nor the finances— nor all the skills necessary— to transform all those things I see into what they could be once more.

But God can make every transformation happen! We may have gone through a tough time... a significant life-challenge... a distressing situation. God can not only rescue us out of that difficulty, but He can restore us to usefulness and beauty once more.

When we go through a distressing time in life, and we choose to keep a right attitude and call out to God, He flies to our rescue. He speaks to us to encourage and comfort us. He reaches down to pull us out of it. He rescues us out of sheer delight. He rewards us. And then, He recreates us so that we can get back to life!

When we are going through these challenging times, we tend to think that— even if we make it out of it— we might be so wounded, or so tired, or so broken that we won't be able to go on. But in those moments, God steps in, restores us and makes us productive for life once more.

You may have been beaten up and broken down, but God knows how to fix what's wrong in your life and make you better than new. He sees all the potential stored up inside you. Invite Him to restore you today!

Scripture To Study: Psalm 18
Key Verse: "He reached down from Heaven and rescued me"
Prayer: *Lord, please restore me today. It's been a tough leg of the journey. I wasn't sure I was going to make it. But I know You can make all things new. Refresh and restore me to usefulness for You. I love You, and...*

DAY 51
FOR THE WEARY

When Jesus said the words we find in Matthew 11:28-30, He was speaking to a crowd. There always seemed to be crowds around Him. No doubt, His message to them that day resonated in their hearts.

I don't know what has caused you to be weary. I don't know why you're worn out or overburdened. I don't know why you are burned out on religion, but what I do know is Jesus simply wants you to walk with Him and talk with Him. He just wants a relationship with you in which the two of you connect and communicate.

Forget about doing for awhile... Focus on being.

Jesus wasn't just speaking to "those people back then" when He said these words. He spoke them for you, for me. He spoke them to let us know that we don't have to walk this road of life alone, carrying a backpack full of cares, concerns, worries, fears, guilt, fatigue, and failure. Instead, He offers to swap loads with us. He offers to show us how to lighten our load in order to enjoy the journey as we walk with Him.

So, while I realize that you may not have a ton of vacation time to stop what you're doing daily and just be, perhaps you can find the time to take today— in the still of the early morning hours, or on a lunch break, or in the quiet of the late night— to just be yourself with Him and let Him give you rest. Not sure where to start? Why not start by simply going back to the these three little verses and let them really sink in? Then pause, and listen with your heart as He speaks to you about how He wants to help you today. It doesn't have to take long, but I'm convinced that if you try it, you'll find that you want to do it more and more each day.

Scripture To Study: Matthew 11:28-30
Key Verse: "Come to Me... and I will give you rest."
Prayer: *Jesus, I am so weary. It feels like I am weighted-down with stress and worry. Please take this load off of me, and give me Your light load. I need Your help today. I love You, and...*

DAY 52
WIND ON THE EMBERS

We live in a wooded area, and if someone sneezes on our property, we have to clean up branches from all the trees around our home. Recently, a terrible storm system went through our area, and we hauled wagon load upon wagon load to our homemade fire pit. We stacked those branches, added a little dryer lint and old sales ads, and whoof... FIRE! Before we went to bed, the fire had burned down, leaving only white-ish gray ash. I checked it. No heat, no flame, no sign of embers. Good, the fire was out.

The next morning, I was out in the yard and noticed a small whiff of gray smoke coming from what was left of a piece of a log in the pit. As I got closer, I noticed a stiff breeze was blowing over some embers in the fire pit which I must have over-looked the night before. There were sticks around the edges of the fire pit which had escaped burning, and so I put a few of them on the embers. As the wind blew, the embers received the oxygen they needed to be fanned back into flame. Fire came alive.

As I put more sticks on the rekindled fire, it occurred to me that this is exactly how God can work in our lives, too. It can look like everything is dead. Over. Done with. Put out. Finished. Yet all it takes is for God to begin blowing His life-giving breath across our lives to revive what is laying hidden inside us.

Scripture tells us that God will give us beauty for ashes. It says that He will not put out a dying flame. God blows on the embers of our lives, not to put out the little burning part that is left, but to fan into flame once more what remains so we can be active and powerful again.

It can happen in an instant. We can feel cold and lifeless one moment, only to burst into a flame-filled life in the next. So don't give up because your life looks like the fire is out. There is a breeze drifting your way. It's building in intensity... and soon you will be, too!

Scripture To Study: Isaiah 61
Key Verse: "He will give a crown of beauty for ashes..."
Prayer: *Dear Lord, blow on the embers of my life with the loving wind of Your Spirit, and breathe life back into me. Take what seems like loss, and make it vibrant again. I love You, and...*

DAY 53
GIVE A CRAYON A CHANCE

Our son, Austin, was doing his schoolwork which involved doing some math so that he could color by number, and he excitedly showed me his skills. I was impressed at how he had stayed in the lines and filled everything in. As I commented on it, he held up a crayon and said that he colored the cardinal in the picture with that crayon. Then he said, "Isn't that funny, Daddy? I thought it was an orange crayon, but it really colors red."

We, too, sometimes get surprised by the crayons (aka, people) we come across in life, don't we? They look like a snob, or a freak, or a geezer... or... or... or. We simply look at their wrapper and their shade, and we make what we think is an educated guess at who they are, what they are like, and what they are capable of. But so often we are wrong, and yet we don't know that we are wrong because we never give them a chance to show their true color.

This has happened for thousands of years. In Scripture, Samuel the prophet was sent by God to Jesse's house to anoint the next king to lead Israel. Jesse presented his sons to Samuel in succession. Samuel thought any of those guys could be the right crayon to color with, but God brought a crayon from out in the field watching sheep who didn't seem to be the right shade or have the right wrapper and told Samuel that he was the one who could rightly color the next page of Israel's history.

Today, let's stop to have that conversation with a person we might not normally talk to. Let's offer that job to someone whose qualifications don't seem to match up on paper. Let's dig a little deeper, actually pick up that crayon and color with it before we determine whether it is what we think is right or not. We just might find ourselves pleasantly surprised like Austin doing his schoolwork.

Scripture To Study: I Samuel 16:1-13
Key Verse: "People judge by outward appearance, but the Lord looks at the heart."
Prayer: *Lord, please forgive me for judging people by my own standards, and please help me to see them the way You do. Give me opportunities today to love like You. I love You, and...*

DAY 54
PANIC OR PEACE?

I was talking with someone recently about our life situation and how we are in a process of discovering "what's next" for us. In the midst of the conversation, I mentioned what a strange sense of peace we have about the Lord having everything under control.

That's when I was reminded of the account in Mark's Gospel, Chapter 4 about Jesus and His disciples in a boat... on the Sea of Galilee... at night... when a storm suddenly blew in out of nowhere. As I thought about that situation, it hit me that we can either have peace in the midst of the panic, or panic in the midst of the peace.

The disciples were freaking out, even though they had the Creator of the world in the boat with them. He was sleeping, even though there was a massive storm raging and all twelve disciples, some experienced fishermen, were freaking out. He had peace in the midst of the panic... they had panic in the presence of the peace.

Truthfully, it's our choice. We can choose to stay at peace despite how crazy things seem to be all around us or we can choose to let go of the control of our emotions and panic despite the fact that we have the Creator of our world right beside us, and He isn't worried a bit. It takes the same amount of energy. It just comes down to who or what we believe is more powerful in our lives... the storm or the Creator.

I believe God will give us His peace to quiet the storm inside us, and I believe that He will speak peace to quiet the storm around us... if we will choose peace over panic. But He lets us choose.

So, c'mon, people... let's choose peace today!

Scripture To Study: Mark 4:35-41

Key Verse: "Jesus was sleeping... The disciples woke Him up, shouting..."

Prayer: *Dear Lord, help me to choose peace instead of panic in the midst of the storms in my life. I know You have power over everything around me, and so I ask You to also take charge of everything in me. I love You, and...*

DAY 55
THE FISH WILL BITE AGAIN

I went fishing. The weather was beautiful. The lake was calm. Between me and my father-in-law we caught... are you ready... count it... one bream. One. Uno. I only got two other nibbles the whole time we were out there. He only got one or two nibbles. And all we caught was one little fish.

We switched lures. We tried live bait. We fished with rods and reels and with jig poles. We tried shallow. We tried deeper. We fished for crappie. We fished for bass. We fished for bream. We pulled up beside other fisherman and asked them how deep they were fishing. We asked them what kind of bait they were using. All of these efforts, and we only caught one small fish. Yet, even before we got the boat back to my in-laws' house, we were already talking about the next time we plan to go fishing.

Just because this fish didn't bite this time doesn't mean they won't bite next time. We've caught fish in that lake and other lakes plenty of times. We're not going to let one disappointment keep us from doing something we love.

And you shouldn't either. Don't quit. Don't give up just because of a "one-off." So things didn't work out the way you planned or hoped. Find the positive. Plan another attempt, and hope again!

In the end, I had a great time with one of my best friends. We enjoyed beautiful weather and God's creation. We laughed and relaxed. Sure, I wanted to load the boat with fish today. So, I'll go again next time because the possibility still exists for it to happen.

There is great possibility still for you as well. Check this day off, and make plans now for making the next time the best time ever. Isn't that the message of hope that Christ brings through the miracles of the great catches of fish? Tried hard and failed? Try once more. The fish will bite again!

Scripture To Study: John 21:1-6
Key Verse: "Throw out your net on the right-hand side of the boat, and you'll get some!"
Prayer: *Jesus, give me courage and faith to try again. Energize my hopes for future success. Help me jettison discouragement and do my best for You. I love You, and...*

DAY 56
WHILE IT WAS STILL DARK

We tried for seven years to have children to no avail. More than one night, we soaked our pillows with tears. More than once we got our hopes up, only to have them dashed. We signed up to adopt, and that wasn't coming together. It was a dark time for me.

During that dark time the Lord brought me to John 20:1 which reads that, "*while it was still dark*," the women came to the tomb. They didn't realize the Son had already risen and they were only moments away from their world springing back into glorious light. The Lord spoke to my heart that morning to let me know that, though it was still dark, the miracle was already in the works for us to have children.

A couple months later, as I headed out to preach at another church, Angela told me to pick up a pregnancy test on the way home. We had a great service, and as promised I picked up a pregnancy test.

Angela took the test the next day and informed me it was positive. Surprised, I bought another test. Again, positive.

We went to the doctor, and in all her years of practice she said she had never seen anyone with levels of positive results so high. God blessed us with our first son, and two years later, with our second son.

We all go through some dark times in life. Times when we think all is lost. It's all over. No hope of things turning around.

But with God, nothing is impossible. Sure it may be dark and you may simply be dutiful at this point, but the miracle is already started. Another few steps and you will find that God was working before you ever knew it! Life will be bright again. Take heart! There will be a day when you tell someone your story like I've told you mine, and you will find it amazing that you ever doubted God.

So, take a few more steps, but may they not be heavy because just a little ahead of you, your miracle awaits your arrival!

Scripture To Study: John 20
Key Verse: "Early Sunday morning, while it was still dark..."
Prayer: *Father, You raised Jesus from the dead. My problem is not too big for You to handle. Please give me faith to hold on. I love You, and...*

DAY 57
VOTED LEAST LIKELY, AND YET...

As high school yearbooks go, there wasn't a whole lot of me in mine. I was smart, but not valedictorian. I didn't play sports, wasn't in the band or the drama department. I didn't work on the yearbook staff, and wasn't prom king. I was normal. Plain. Vanilla.

Some high school yearbooks contain a list of "most likely to..." candidates. You know... most likely to succeed... most likely to be a movie star... most likely to get arrested... and so on. But I was not chosen "most likely" to be or do anything. I was more "least likely."

It's why I find it interesting the first person Jesus chose to show Himself to after rising from the dead was... wait for it... Mary Magdalene, everyone! Cricket, cricket. Wait a minute. Why her?

She wasn't one of the main disciples. She's a woman, and men were still favored in society. Then there's that whole demon-possessed past thing. Surely, He could have chosen someone more reputable. John was with Him through His darkest hours. He gave John care of His mother. John was part of the inner circle. Yet Jesus chose instead to show His resurrected Self to a "least likely."

In my heart, I believe He chose her precisely *because* she was on the "least likely" list. Perhaps she needed to be the first to see Him so that rest of us "least likelies" could know that we matter to Him.

Maybe you feel like you've been overlooked in life. Maybe you don't feel like you measure up to others in any category. Maybe you think you might get the "least likely" trophy... if they were giving one.

I have good news for you today. Jesus comes to the least likely and makes them unforgettable! As long as the story of Jesus coming back to life is told, so the name of Mary Magdalene will be tied to it. I hope that fact gives you hope... hope that He will come to you, choose you, and tie you to Himself forever.

Scripture To Study: John 20:11-18
Key Verse: "'Dear woman, why are you crying?' Jesus asked her."
Prayer: *Dear Lord, I may not seem like much to others, but I am glad that You make me worthy. Thank You for Your love, Your grace and Your power at work in my life. I love You, and...*

DAY 58
ARE YOU A SYNDICATION SUCCESS?

Two great occurrences took place in 1970... I was born, and *The Brady Bunch* launched its first season on prime time television. I'm still around... and so are the Brady's. Although, my guess is that a few more people know about *The Brady Bunch* than know about me. In fact, if I asked you to describe at least one episode, I bet you could do it.

The Brady Bunch ran five seasons from 1969-1974, and it was never a successful show as far as the numbers reflected at the time. However, it ran long enough to cross the threshold to be put into syndication, and since September 1975 when it launched its first re-runs in syndication, it has aired somewhere in the United States every day. At this point, that is more than four decades... running 365 days per year without fail. Yet it wasn't deemed successful enough to keep on the air. Think about that. At the time, it didn't appear to have staying power. My kids are now watching it on DVD for the first time, and they are hooked... despite not knowing what a rotary dial telephone or a reel-to-reel tape recorder are. They laugh at the funny scenes. They get the point of the parental teaching moments. They love it.

In I Samuel 16:7, God points out that Samuel should let God do the picking and choosing about who will be successful. And He lets Samuel know that He (God) doesn't look at people the same way people do. He looks at the heart and not outward appearances.

So, if today you don't feel you qualify as a success, let me ask you this... Whose standard are you using to measure yourself?

Albert Einstein said, "Everybody is a genius. But if you judge a fish by its ability to climb a tree, it will live its whole life believing it is stupid." Sometimes we allow ourselves to be measured by the wrong measuring stick. Choose instead to live your life by God's measure. Who knows? You may just turn out to be a success in syndication.

Scripture To Study: I Samuel 16:1-13
Key Verse: "The Lord has not chosen any of these."
Prayer: *Dear Lord, please help me to view myself and others in the way You do. Help me to trust Your estimation. I love You, and...*

DAY 59
ALWAYS

Trampoline. Swingset. Pool. See-saw. Bikes.

There was a time in our lives when we wondered if we would ever have the privilege of having children in our family, and thus the joy of a yard filled with activities. There were plenty of nights we soaked our pillows with tears.

But God had promised, and we held onto that promise. Admittedly, some days we had great faith. Other days we wondered if that promise would ever be fulfilled.

But God had promised, and we know His Word says that He always keeps His promises.

In some ways, I wish we could have seen then what our life looks like now with two fun, handsome, strong, growing boys in it. I guess that's not really having faith, though. At the time, all we could do was hope... and trust... and pray... and take Him at His Word.

Surprisingly, from time to time, we find ourselves in similar situations... you know, needing to take Him at His Word when it hasn't actually happened yet. Truth be told, it still isn't a whole lot easier now. At least until I look at those two miracles playing in the front yard, hollering for me to come play with them. At a moment like that, I am reminded that...

God... *ALWAYS*... keeps... His... promises!

So, if you're going through your own time in life when you wonder if God is actually going to do what He said, take heart and take note. You're just as special to Him as we are. If He did it for us, He'll do it for you. It's not about us. It's about His character. You can count on him because... God *always* keeps His promises!

Scripture To Study: Psalm 138
Key Verse: "... for Your promises are backed by all the honor of Your name."
Prayer: *Father, I thank You that I can trust You. Thank You for being reliable and always keeping Your promises. I need Your help today to trust some more in this new challenge in life. I love You, and...*

DAY 60
A PLACE CALLED "NOWHERE"

We have some friends who give at least one scholarship each year to a teenager who wants to go on a missions trip but is financially challenged. Their story about how the scholarship came about precious, and it is theirs to tell.

Several years ago, I found out about the scholarship and knew of a student going on a trip I was leading who needed some assistance. I obtained the application and gave it to the student who subsequently filled it out and sent it to our friends. The student ended up receiving the scholarship that year and went on the missions trip with us.

When I thanked our friends for helping this student, the wife said something so profound that I am often reminded of it. She wrote that they were happy to be able to help and then added these words...

People like to thank God for blessings that seem to come out of nowhere... and I'm so glad I live in a place called "Nowhere!"

I read those words and was floored. For what seemed like the first time in my life, it hit me that God uses average, everyday, ordinary people like you and me to share His blessings with others.

That scholarship. A check in the mail. Someone in the drive-thru ahead of you buying your coffee. Those blessings didn't come from nowhere. They came from a real God, utilizing a real person to impact your life positively at a moment when you least expected it.

Now flip it. Just think... you and I live in a place called "Nowhere." Each day we have the potential to transform someone else's day by blessing them. It doesn't have to be just with money. Pay a compliment. Pay respect. Send a note. Send flowers. Send a text.

Someone within your reach tomorrow will be within your capacity to bless. They may think their blessing came from nowhere... but you will know that you are a resident there!

Scripture To Study:　　Galatians 6:1-10
Key Verse:　　"... we should do good to everyone..."
Prayer: *Dear Lord, please help me to take every opportunity to bless and help others. Let me live in that place called "Nowhere" by loving, encouraging and inspiring others for You. I love You, and...*

THE UPSIDE

DAY 61
YES, YOU CAN

There are times when my boys tell me that they can't do something. That bothers me on those occasions when I absolutely know for a fact that they *can* do whatever it is they think they cannot accomplish. I suppose that's because when I have listened to or read material written by former Navy Seals, there is a recurring theme which comes up...

When Seals are trained, they are taught that most people think they are finished and therefore quit at 60% of their actual capacity. Thus, you still have 40% in your tank to keep going and finish strong.

You and I, well, we can do more than we think we can typically. If we will push past the mental and emotional barriers we have set for ourselves, we can do a lot more.

You can put up with your boss longer than you think. You can be kinder than you think. You can save more money than you think. You can extend more grace to your child than you think.

We all have challenges we're facing in life. I've got mine. You've got yours. We all wish life was easy all the time, but it's not. The thing is, we don't have to tackle this on our own.

Paul wrote to some deeply challenged believers in Philippi and told them that it's possible to do "all things" through Christ Who strengthens us. That's even more than the Navy Seals claim! In other words, no matter what you come up against, if you'll keep Jesus Christ involved in your life, there won't be anything too difficult for you to overcome. The Seals talk about giving 100%. With Jesus, we are able to do everything *He* can do through us.

So, let's do a few more push-ups and eat a few less sweets. Let's give a little more. Let's help a little more. Let's complain a little less. In fact, let's just remove the word "can't" from our vocabulary. Let's give it all we have... and then some!!!

Scripture To Study: Philippians 4:10-14
Key Verse: "For I can do everything through Christ..."
Prayer: *Jesus, I don't feel like I can handle it today. Please help me sense Your power and supernatural ability at work in me. I know that, with You, nothing is impossible. I love You, and...*

DAY 62
GRILLED CHEESE AND CHOPSTICKS

From age 1 to age 7, my family lived in a Minnesota town across from Fargo, North Dakota. Fargo was bigger, and so it was not uncommon for us to go there to shop or eat. One day while in Fargo, we ate at our favorite Chinese restaurant. Mom and Dad ordered Moo Goo Gai Pan, and I ordered a grilled cheese sandwich.

Our food was served, and soon Mom and Dad began to hear murmurs and giggles coming from tables around us. They saw people pointing at our table. Then they realized people were pointing at me. By the time they turned around to see why, I had my entire grilled cheese sandwich suspended in mid-air between my plate and my mouth, with one chopstick in each of my small fists stabbed into the middle of the grilled cheese. It was beginning to tilt out of balance, and that is what had all the onlookers gawking. Finally, with great effort, I got a bite. People chuckled and cheered, and then I was very clearly instructed by my parents that this was not proper etiquette.

No one came to eat that day expecting to see a kid eat a grilled cheese with chopsticks. It just isn't what you do. Yet sadly, we let that type mentality dictate far too much of our lives.

God doesn't always do things the way people expect. His Word says His ways aren't like our ways, and our thoughts aren't like His thoughts. His Word says He is doing something new. New means you and I haven't seen it before. Who knows what amazing, creative and unexpected ideas He has cooked up to bless you? Ask yourself this question... When was the last time you invited God to do something new in your life?

Let's not be content with a life of eating grilled cheese sandwiches with our hands. Grab those proverbial chopsticks, and let God do something new in you! Who knows? You might just enjoy it... and bring joy to a lot of folks around you.

Scripture To Study: Isaiah 55
Key Verse: "My ways are far beyond anything you could imagine"
Prayer: *Father, infuse me with Your creativity. Do something new and wonderful in me. Surprise me with joy today, and let that joy spill out into the lives of others for Your glory. I love You, and...*

DAY 63
OH, IT'S GONNA HAPPEN

It's like our son, Austin, cannot even imagine the possibility of a negative outcome when he is wanting and believing for something. He sees a toy or game that he absolutely has to have, and he begins to tell us about it. As he describes it in detail, he says things like, "When I get it, I'm going to..." Not "if I get it," mind you, but "When I get it."

In his mind, there is no possible way we would say "no" to his request. He is innocent and full of faith in not only our *ability* to provide what he wants, but also in our *willingness* to bring him joy.

He entered a contest recently in which he has the possibility of winning an iPad mini. In his mind, he has already won. He just has to wait for the contest to come to a close and receive his prize. He doesn't consider that other kids might also have a chance to win. The odds mean nothing to him... because, in his mind, he is destined to win.

Oh, that I would view my Heavenly Father with such childlike faith! Oh, to be able to completely exclude any possibility that God would not answer my request. Oh, that I would never view failure as a possible outcome, and envision only success.

Yet, isn't that what Jesus instructed His disciples to do... to have faith like a child? What a radical concept that must have been for them. What a radical concept it often is for me.

God is a good Father. Surely, I can count on Him to come through for me. There is no reasonable explanation for my doubting. I will win! I will receive! I will be filled with joy, because He laughs with me... and loves me... and lavishes blessings on me.

Of course He does. Why would I think otherwise? For the record, He feels exactly the same way about you. So put on your faith like Austin today, and believe for the best to come your way!

Scripture To Study: Matthew 7:7-11
Key Verse: "...how much more will your Heavenly Father give good gifts to those who ask Him."
Prayer: *Heavenly Father, You have never caused me to doubt Your goodness and faithfulness toward me. Please give me every blessing of Heaven You have stored up for me today. I love You, and...*

DAY 64
VOTE EARLY AND OFTEN

In Louisiana, we have a funny statement we use when we encourage people to cast their vote… We say, "Vote early, and vote often!" It's a joke nowadays, but I'm sure there was probably a period in time when it was an actual practice. People made their choice, again and again… and then again.

The truth is, we each have the opportunity every day to vote early and vote often. We have the privilege to choose kindness or unkindness. To smile at people or glare at them. To speak words which build them up or tear them down. There are two candidates which produce two very different outcomes, and it seems like the choice should be crystal clear. Yet, we seem to struggle to decide.

Each morning when we wake up, we have to decide all over again which lever we will pull. The opportunity and responsibility is presented to us regularly… Traffic jam? Time to vote. Someone in the store rude to you? Time to vote. Tough day at work? Time to vote. Kids misbehaving? Time to vote.

The Apostle Paul writes that our lives are never free from this kind of choice… the choice between being led by the Holy Spirit, or being led by our own self-nature. It was a choice that Adam and Eve made every day. And it is a choice we each still make all throughout every day of each of our lives.

At the retirement celebration for Rev. Joe Granberry, former Superintendent for the South Texas Assemblies of God, one of the speakers said of him, "When he walks into a room, he changes the atmosphere." To quote the Sidewalk Prophets, "I want to live like that!" By simply treating others the way God treats us, we can change hearts, change minds, and change situations! What if we began to spread kindness on social media and in daily conversations? What if we were kind at home, at work and around our community? What if we voted early and often for kindness?

Scripture To Study: Galatians 5:16-26
Key Verse: "These two forces are constantly fighting each other…"
Prayer: *Holy Spirit, please help me today to vote early and often to live in the love and kindness You have shown to me. I love You, and…*

DAY 65
HOW MUCH MORE?

We don't mind giving our boys things they want. I'm not talking about spoiling them. I'm saying that we listen to what they talk about and have a pretty good idea at most times what they are interested in. So, as long as it's not something ridiculous or something that would hurt them, we like getting those things for them.

Good parents want to bless their kids. That's really why they want their kids to behave... to do right... to go along with them as parents... to express love and appreciation to them as parents. It's not because the parents are needy or demanding, but because, if the kids will do these things, it will make it much easier for the parents to bless them and not have to correct or punish them instead.

Now, if we, as earthly parents who admittedly do not have it all together, want to put a smile on our kids faces by blessing them with some of the things they want, why do we have such a difficult time believing that our Heavenly Father wants to put a smile on our faces as His kids?

This is why He gives us guidelines to follow in life. He wants us to do right so that He is free to bless us as His children. So maybe it is time we adjust our view of the commandments in Scripture from a list of do's and don'ts which we must keep in order to earn God's approval to a view that sees them as a way of living which draws us into a closer relationship with Him and which creates an atmosphere in which He is free to bless us.

Let me just add that, while we don't live for the blessings God gives us, it's also not wrong to want those blessings and ask Him for them as we follow Him with our whole heart. I know our boys don't think twice about asking us... and we don't mind one bit. Neither will He.

Scripture To Study: Exodus 20:1-17
Key Verse: "Then you will live a long, full life in the land..."
Prayer: *Lord, please help me today to see Your commands as the path to my blessing instead of keeping me from good things. I trust You as my Heavenly Father to put a smile on my face. I love You, and...*

DAY 66
TAKE IT OR LEAVE IT?

Recently, my sister and I were discussing the process of moving her stuff from one house to another, and she said something which struck a chord with me on a couple different levels. She said something along the lines of, "It's like you have to tell yourself, 'I really don't need to take that with me into a new home.'"

It caught my attention because in our last move, PR31 and I had said many times while packing that we didn't want to take certain things to the new home. We would rather get rid of it there before we moved because it didn't fit in our new setting.

But it thundered through my synapses on a whole different levers as well. You see, all of us face times in life when we segue from one phase of life into another. Maybe it's a change in jobs... or location... or relationships. And we need to ask ourselves if there are some things which should be left behind. We need to identify those things which do not need to be brought into a new setting.

Perhaps it's an attitude which you need to get rid of so that you can move forward in a relationship. Maybe it's unforgiveness you need to sell in your relational garage sale before you can move forward into the next phase of your career. Or maybe it's a habit you need to toss in the trash so you can move forward into the next level of life.

Whatever the issue, hang-up, attitude, feelings, chip on your shoulder, the hurt, the guilt, the shame... whatever it is, leave it behind. You really don't need to pack it up and take it with you. It's not going to fit in with what "the next" in your life looks like. In fact, it might actually hinder you from being able to move forward into what is next.

So jettison what won't work from where you are now, and get ready to find the new where you're headed. Trust me, you'll be glad you did. You'll enter the new less weary and more free!

Scripture To Study: Philippians 3:12-14
Key Verse: "Forgetting the past and looking forward..."
Prayer: *Father, please help me today to see those parts of my life which are no longer of value to me and which I need to leave behind. I want to be free to go new places with You. I love You, and...*

DAY 67
FROM FEAR TO FUN

When we first got into the pool at my sister's house that day Austin did not even want to put his whole face under water. Dunking his entire head under water seemed an unthinkable challenge he wanted to overcome, but had not yet. He said he just couldn't do it.

Then it happened. As we kept encouraging him and giving him opportunities, we could see his desire growing. We practiced holding breath. Soon, his whole face was under. Then only the crown of his head was out of the water.

What he had once feared became fun, and in what seemed like just a moment's time, he was sitting on the bottom of the pool. He would pop up out of the water and excitedly say, "Watch me, Daddy! Look what I can do!" And down he would go.

Joy replaced fear. Confidence overcame caution. His skills instantly multiplied, and he began swimming and twirling under water.

That night before bed, Austin looked at me and said, "Daddy, wouldn't be cool if I could jump off the side of the pool and do two backflips in the air before I went into the water?" Who was this fish who had replaced my son? I know this... I love to see another fear vanquished in his life so he can enjoy the full life God has for him.

And what about you? What fear is it which has you held captive, preventing you from enjoying that abundant life? What is whispering in your ear that you can't overcome it?

God doesn't create fear or cause fear in us. God gives us the power we need to overcome it. He gives us an abundant life to enjoy.

Whatever your fears today, Austin would be quick to tell you to push past them because it is so much fun on the other side. Now he's free to enjoy something he didn't think he was able to before. You will be, too! Just hold your breath... and go for it!!!

Scripture To Study: 2 Timothy 1:3-7
Key Verse: "For God has not given us a spirit of fear..."
Prayer: *Dear Lord, thank You for giving me a spirit of power, love and a sound mind. I believe it, receive it and act upon it today. Help me to live the abundant life You have for me. I love You, and...*

DAY 68
THE CHECK IS IN THE MAIL

Countless sermons have been preached from it. I have both been comforted by it myself and quoted it to offer comfort to others. Apart from John 3:16, Psalm 23 may be the most widely known and most beloved passage from Scripture ever. Since it has such power to encourage, comfort, and lift, let's focus our attention on The Good Shepherd of Psalm 23... and I hope we find our hearts drawn to Him as we go along.

David, a shepherd writing a song about God from a perspective he understands, paints a portrait of a God who loves us and looks out for our best interest. The first truth about God he points out is that God is the ultimate Provider.

I have been given one of those handshakes when someone slips you a $20 bill or a $100 bill in a time of need. We have received a check in the mail when we didn't know where the money was going to come from to pay bills. I've also had work provided when I needed income.

And whether through work or gift, I have learned that God the Good Shepherd always provides for His sheep. Not just financially, either. Psalm 23, verses 1-3 point out that the Good Shepherd provides not only our daily normal human requirements, but also our rest, peace, and emotional well-being.

The point is that He knows what we need, and He provides it. With God as your Shepherd, your every need is supplied.

It's a great thing to be provided for. As kids, we don't usually understand all that our parents do to provide for us. But as we get older and begin having to provide for ourselves or our own family, we begin to grasp how much they provided. As God's kids, we are completely provided for.

If you feel like you are lacking something today, ask the Good Shepherd. He knows how to provide for your every need.

Scripture To Study: Psalm 23
Key Verse: "The Lord is my shepherd; I have everything I need."
Prayer: *Good Shepherd, I have this need I cannot meet on my own. Please come through for me and supply for it. I trust You. I believe that You will give me what I need. I love You, and...*

DAY 69
DIRECTIONALLY CHALLENGED

I used to be horribly directionally challenged. For example, I once took over driving responsibilities on a vacation trip after stopping along the way to eat. We got back in the vehicle— I in the driver's seat and my father-in-law, the person who actually knew how to get where we were going, in the passenger seat— and we headed out.

He leaned back his seat to take a nap, and I drove like the wind... in the wrong direction! It was pre-GPS days, people. Give me a break. When he woke up thirty minutes later, he sat up, looked around and mentioned that something didn't look right. He had made that trip numerous times, and he could tell all was not as it should be.

When he asked me which way I turned as we headed out and I described it, we all realized what had happened. I went the wrong way because I was not familiar with the journey. That little mishap cost us an extra hour of drive time and a little extra fuel on a vacation trip. It also cost me some good-natured ribbing for several years.

Now, that was a little frustrating during that trip, but not knowing which path to take on the journey of life... well, that misstep could cost us dearly. It's why I'm so glad David let us know in the 23rd Psalm that the Good Shepherd— aka, God, the One who actually knows which direction we need to go every time— not only *provides* for us, but He also *points* us in the right direction.

Verses 2 and 3 say that He leads us to what we most need, and He guides us along the right paths if we will just follow Him. David also writes in Psalm 37 that God even directs our steps, those smaller parts of the bigger journey.

Today, if you need guidance and direction on this leg of the journey in your life, commit to follow Jesus, the Good Shepherd. He won't steer you wrong. He won't even take a nap along the way.

Scripture To Study: Psalm 23
Key Verse: "He guides me along right paths..."
Prayer: *Good Shepherd, I have to make decisions today, and I need Your help in making them. Please lead me and guide me along the right paths for my life. I love You, and...*

DAY 70
GUARD DUTY

Call it a dream. Call it a vision. Call it a figment of my imagination. Call it whatever you want. I know what I saw.

PR31 and I were serving as lead pastors at a church in northeast Louisiana. God was doing great things in peoples' lives. The church was growing and getting healthy. And the devil was not happy.

We began to be bombarded by various fears, and it became apparent to us that this was not natural. It was something spiritual.

I remember waking up one night in such fear, like there was "someone" or "something" in the house, and it wasn't a human. I recall being afraid in the darkness, but I also knew the Good Shepherd was keeping watch over us. So I asked Him to help us. I explained our fears and let Him know that we really needed Him to protect us.

At that moment, I leaned out of bed and glanced down the hallway of the 80-foot doublewide mobile home. What I saw almost startled me just before it instilled a great sense of comfort. Standing in the hallway in full battle armor was another "being" I somehow knew was on our side. I could only see up to his chest because his head and shoulders were higher than the eight-foot ceiling. He was obviously not restricted by natural barriers, and he was on guard duty in our home.

Then I saw another similar being at our front door. Comfort washed over me in that moment. The Good Shepherd was showing me "His rod and His staff" were protecting me from any harm which the enemy might try to bring our way. From that time on, we did not struggle with fear in the same way.

The Good Shepherd not only *provides* and *points*, but He also *protects* us from the attack of the enemy of our souls. No matter how dark the valley, the Good Shepherd has us covered.

If you're battling fear today, ask the Good Shepherd to protect you and comfort you. He won't let you down.

Scripture To Study: Psalm 23
Key Verse: "Your rod and staff protect and comfort me."
Prayer: *Good Shepherd, thank You for always protecting me. Please take away my fears today, and keep me close to You. I love You, and...*

DAY 71
BAM! HOW 'BOUT THAT?

Here's the thing you have to know... There is a real devil, and he is opposed to you simply because God values you and wants you in His forever family. The devil and his wicked imps are your enemies.

Here's the other thing you need to know... They may be your enemies, but God is the Good Shepherd, and your enemies are no match for Him. It's not even close. He has no competition. God is in a league of His own. The devil is not the equal opposite of God. He is a defeated enemy gasping for his last breath.

So when David writes about God as the Ultimate Shepherd in Psalm 23, he writes from an experienced perspective. David was a shepherd, too. He defeated lions and bears with a stick and his bare hands. So he didn't mind taking his sheep out each day and making sure they had a good meal right in the area where enemies lurked... because he knew how to handle those enemies.

And God knows perfectly well how to vanquish your enemies. I like God's moxie. His bravado. His flair for thumbing His nose in the face of the enemy. David says that God basically sets the table for a feast, makes us the guest of honor and blesses us... right in front of our enemies. And they can't do a single thing about it because He's standing right there beside us, ever vigilant!

So eat in peace today. Enjoy God's blessings today. Let God honor you today as you stay close to Him. Don't let the enemy give you an ounce of worry or concern. They can skulk around the perimeter as you are blessed and honored, but they can't stop it.

JoAnna Gaines once made a sign on one of the *Fixer Upper* TV episodes which read, "It's a good day for a good day." I would tweak it a little to read, "It's a good day to belong to the Good Shepherd!" Today, let Him *prepare* a feast for you... as the Devil can only watch!

Scripture To Study: Psalm 23
Key Verse: "...in the presence of my enemies."
Prayer: *Good Shepherd, help me remember today that no weapon formed against me will prosper because You have chosen to bless me. Thank you for honoring me and blessing me! I love You, and...*

DAY 72
LOCKED-ON

I looked left, then right. In that moment, I estimated my small pickup's ability, my driving skills, the speed of oncoming vehicles, and I calculated that I could pull out of the parking lot and onto the street with time and space to spare. So I stepped on the accelerator, and I was right.

However, the guy in the bigger pick-up truck which I pulled out in front of disagreed. He yelled, shook his fist, and blew his horn. When we got to a stoplight, he got out of his vehicle, and I got scared. The light turned green, and I took off.

I felt like I was driving for my life in an action movie. The guy just kept following me. I drove all over, making U-turns, taking back roads, speeding up, and slowing down. No matter what I did, I couldn't shake this guy. I finally decided to go home, hoping to get into the house before he could get out of his truck and pummel me into cookie crumbs.

I made it into my driveway, but I wasn't fast enough. Before I got inside, he pulled into the driveway, jumped out of his truck and began yelling as he headed toward me. Scared silly, I was very apologetic. Fortunately, he was all bark and no bite. He finally had enough cussing and correcting me, and took off. I stood there shaking because I had not been able to shake this guy.

David closes out the 23rd Psalm by highlighting a somewhat similar, amazing character trait of the Good Shepherd... namely that God's goodness and unfailing love... much like the guy whom I couldn't shake... follow us constantly! Only God's goodness and unfailing love don't create fear or intimidation. Instead they *pursue* us in order to bring us blessing.

The point is that we can't shake God's goodness off our trail. For His sheep, the Good Shepherd's goodness and unfailing love are like heat-seeking missiles which have locked-on to their target and eventually catch up. That's a lot better than being chased by an angry guy in a pick-up... and I would know!

Scripture To Study: Psalm 23
Key Verse: "Surely Your goodness and unfailing love... pursue me"
Prayer: *Good Shepherd, lock on to my life with your goodness and unfailing love. I need them in a big way today. I love You, and...*

THE UPSIDE

DAY 73
A LINE IN THE SAND

A good portion of my childhood, my teens, and half my twenties were spent in Texas. Kids in Texas are taught Texas history with pride. That's because The Republic of Texas has a captivating history from which powerful lessons can be mined.

For example, at one point in its struggle for freedom, the Texas army was holed-up in a Spanish mission in San Antonio commonly known now as "The Alamo." 5,000 Mexican troops surrounded them. The Texan military leadership had sent a request for reinforcements, but none could come. When Colonel William Barrett Travis realized this, he made a decision in his own heart and mind that this is where he would make his final stand.

Travis gathered the entire force, gave a speech about their peril and how they could give time for the rest of the Texan army to win. Then he laid the tip of his sword on the sandy ground and dragged it several feet, leaving a line in its wake. He told the soldiers that they could leave now and no one would think any less of them. Only one man, some women and the children left that night. The rest stepped across the line and so sealed their fate... as well as their place in history.

The miniature Texan force was ultimately overwhelmed 13 days later by General Santa Anna's juggernaut. Their battle, though it appeared a loss, did indeed set up a victory for the rest of Texas.

Any person who is going to do something significant in life faces "line in the sand" moments when they choose to go forward and not look back. The Apostle Paul had such an experience with Jesus on the road outside Damascus. Later, in his letter to the church at Philippi, Paul writes that he has stepped across the line in the sand.

Let's choose to step across those lines into greatness today! Let's not look back! Like Colonel William Barrett Travis and the Apostle Paul, let's forge into the unknown with only a knowing that what may come may be challenging, but it will also be worthwhile... and we will never be forgotten for our commitment!

Scripture To Study: Philippians 3:12-4:1
Key Verse: "...forgetting the past and looking forward..."
Prayer: *Dear Lord, please help me do something great for You. You have made me for greatness. I will not shrink back. I love You, and...*

DAY 74
NEED SOME LIGHT?

Years ago, like B.C. (before children), we rented a house in Pigeon Forge, Tennessee for a week. One night, I woke up and needed to visit the facilities. I didn't want to wake Angela and decided to navigate the trip in the dark. Relieved and quite sleepy, as I turned to exit the bathroom, my whole world suddenly came crashing to the floor. I stumbled, and my shin hit something solid. As my body lurched forward, my face slammed into something metal, and my nose exploded in pain. This was followed by my face sliding down a wall of some type, ending with me in a heap on the floor, groaning and a little damp. I couldn't figure out where I was or what had happened. That is, until the light came on when PR31 came rushing in to see what was wrong.

In my semi-comatose state, I had forgotten we were on vacation... in a different house. I had turned to the leave the bathroom where our bathroom's door normally was. The only problem is that where the door was in our house was where the shower stall was in this house. I had stepped on the ledge at the base, tripped, hit my shin on the base, slammed my nose into the hot or cold knob, slid down the fiberglass wall and landed in a pile at the still damp floor of the shower. The truth is... I just needed light. Even a small nightlight would have done the trick. Light would have pointed out where I needed to go.

We all walk into some dark spots in life. We're not really sure where we are or how to get where we need to go. We need light. We need someone outside of ourselves who can bring light to the situation so that we don't stumble, fall, and hurt ourselves anymore. We need God.

Isaiah wrote in Isaiah 42:16... "...I will turn their darkness into light...". God wants to shine the light in your dark places today. In fact, He's promised to do it! Don't stumble around any longer.

Scripture To Study: Isaiah 42:10-17
Key Verse: "I will brighten the darkness before them..."
Prayer: *Father, please bring light to the dark places in my life. Help me to know what I should do and say. I thank You for Your promises to smooth out the way ahead of me. I love You, and...*

DAY 75
SUPER GUIDE

Awhile back, Alex and Austin discovered on their Super Mario Bro's game that there is a mode called "Super Guide" in which the computer takes over and completes a course perfectly without any mistakes. At any point, they can take back over from Super Guide and keep playing themselves.

So, they do what they can do on the game and then hand it off to this "Super Guide" to handle what they can't. In fact, those crazy guys will sometimes let the Super Guide play an entire level, get to the end, and then they take control back just in time to claim the flag at the end and complete the course.

About the time I begin to think that isn't really fair, I also begin to think to myself that this is exactly what God does for us. Didn't Jesus say that He would ask the Father, and the Father would send us the Holy Spirit to be a "Super Guide" who would help us through all the difficulties of life?

So often, having done what I can do and facing something I cannot seem to accomplish on my own, I turn to my Super Guide and ask Him to get me through to complete that leg of my course. And while He does all the work, He let's me claim the victory flag. It may look like I've done it, but really He did all the heavy lifting.

I'm glad I have the Holy Spirit as my Super Guide. I couldn't do this life on my own successfully. Today, I just want to take this moment to give Him the credit for overcoming all my obstacles, defeating all my opposition and making me a winner.

If you look at your life today and find yourself struggling to overcome, why not ask the ultimate Super Guide to help you succeed as well? He knows how to help you win in life!

Scripture To Study: John 16:5-15
Key Verse: "When the Spirit of truth comes, He will guide you..."
Prayer: *Holy Spirit, please give me the wisdom, knowledge, understanding, insight and guidance I need to live a Christ-honoring life. I need Your help to navigate the challenges I face. I love You, and...*

DAY 76
97%

All I remembered about Christopher Columbus until recently was that he is credited with discovering North America. Although he wasn't really the first person to do so, and the fact that it really wasn't what he was trying to accomplish. But I learned more than ever before about this intriguing man's life as we taught our boys about him last week.

One of the craziest facts I learned was that his crew almost mutinied on him. They had been at sea, with no land at all in sight, for two months. Afraid for their lives and tired of believing in something that did not seem to be real, they wanted to turn back.

Columbus convinced them to give him three more days. Then, if they had not found land, he agreed to turn back with them. On the evening of the second day, land was sighted, and the rest is history.

But think about this... Those men had traveled *two months*, and yet they were prepared to give up and turn back, when they were only *two days* away from achieving one of the greatest feats of their time. They had completed 97% of the journey. All they had to do was go a little farther. But because they couldn't see their goal even through a spyglass yet, their hearts were weary.

Perhaps you are weary today. You've been trying to do the right thing, but you're tired. Tired of not seeing the end result.

The Apostle Paul wrote to some people who felt like giving up and told them what Columbus told his crew... Don't give up! You're almost there. The hardest part is behind you. Just a little more. Stay on the journey. You will soon find that your continued persistence, commitment and faithfulness have paid off. You'll be glad you didn't give up when you had 97% behind you and only 3% to go.

Don't mutiny on God today. Hoist the sails a few more times. Keep the spyglass to your eye. Be encouraged... I have a sense that land is not as far away as you might think!

Scripture To Study: Galatians 6:9
Key Verse: "So let's not get tired of doing what is good."
Prayer: *Dear Lord, I don't feel like I can keep going. I'm tired of trying, but I'm willing to go on with Your help. I love You, and...*

DAY 77
YOU'RE JOKING, RIGHT?

One of my favorite movies of all time is... *Rocketman*. In it, Harland Williams plays the bumbling, and yet brilliant, Fred Z. Randall who, through a series of ridiculous events, ends up on the first manned mission to Mars. Once clear of earth's orbit, Fred accidentally ends up on a world-wide broadcast of a video call between the President and the astronauts. The President asks Fred what it's like up in space, and Fred replies, "From up here, the earth looks like a giant blueberry."

What Fred portrayed in that scene is a known fact for all of us alive today... the earth is round. But when Columbus lived, many people did not believe that now well-known fact. In fact, most people during Columbus' life believed the world was flat.

Yet Columbus believed the earth was round. He was wrong about much of what he thought, but he was right about believing the earth is round. He believed so strongly that, although it took him many attempts to gain the financial backing and actually find a crew who didn't think they would fall off the edge of the earth by sailing too far, he persisted.

That's what faith does. Faith motivates us in the face of doubt. C. S. Lewis wrote, "When the whole world is running towards a cliff, he who runs in the opposite direction appears to have lost his mind."

Hebrews 11:1 tells us, "Faith is the confidence that what we hope for will actually happen; it gives us assurance about things we cannot see." And just five verses later, the writer of that letter tells us that it is impossible to please God without faith.

So ignore the naysayers today. Run the opposite direction when you know in your heart God has promised you that you are running the right way. Be willing to test that of which God has assured you. And one day we will be celebrating *your* accomplishments!

Scripture To Study: Hebrews 11
Key Verse: "And it is impossible to please God without faith."
Prayer: *Lord, sometimes it feels like I'm the only person going in the direction in which I sense You leading me. I know what You have promised, and I want to please You. Please help me keep on in the right direction. I love You, and...*

DAY 78
THE UNKNOWN

Christopher Columbus lived an adventurous, astounding, amazing life, but he probably didn't realize it. His life ended with him mostly a lonely and forgotten man. Many discredited his efforts. Few wanted to be his friend. Most people failed to recognize his significance during during his lifetime. Yet he had inspired and emboldened countless new explorers.

In the end, Columbus thought he had accomplished one amazing thing, when in reality he had accomplished something far greater. He died thinking he had found a way by sea to Asia, but he had really discovered trade winds leading to an area of the world which was on the verge of discovery. Columbus died not knowing the significant impact he had made on people who would sail in his wake.

Matthew 26 gives us the account of a woman who crashes a dinner party and pours out expensive perfume, probably the most expensive and precious object she owned, on Jesus. Some misunderstood. Most did not realize her significance. But Jesus said, "*I tell you the truth, wherever the Good News is preached throughout the world, this woman's deed will be remembered and discussed.*"

I'm sure that woman didn't realize what a big deal she was at the time. Kind of like Columbus. Kind of like you or me. I'm guessing that, even as you read this, you truly do not realize that you are impacting the lives of so many people in such a massive way. You most likely have no clue about what your real accomplishments are. You probably don't recognize your long-term impact.

People may not recognize your contribution right now. Sail on anyway! You may not be as popular as someone else. Pour perfume anyway! You may not get everything right, but live your life to the fullest for the Lord. There will come a day— perhaps when you are old or have even passed on— when people will tell the stories of your greatness, and you will be remembered for all that you achieved.

Scripture To Study: Matthew 26:6-13
Key Verse: "...this woman's deed will be remembered..."
Prayer: *Lord, I want to make an impact for You, whether I or others recognize it in my lifetime. Please help me. I love You, and...*

DAY 79
ENOUGH FOR TODAY

Anne Shirley Cuthbert says to her friend Diana in *Anne of Green Gables*, "Isn't it nice to think that tomorrow is a brand new day with no mistakes yet?" I don't recall Diana's response, but I know mine... YES!!!

I try to follow Jesus wholeheartedly, do right, be good, help others, love and lead my family, but I am glad that tomorrow brings with it a fresh start. I cannot undo my yesterdays, but I resonate with Anne's question. It reminds me of what the prophet Jeremiah wrote in the Old Testament book of Lamentations... "*The steadfast love of the Lord never ceases; His mercies never come to an end; they are new every morning; great is Your faithfulness.*" No matter how yesterday went, the Lord loves us and gives us hope for today.

Bad day at work yesterday? Get up, get dressed and go back to the office or worksite because He's giving you new mercies for today!

Feeling like a lousy parent for mishandling a situation with your kids at a crucial moment? Roll out of bed, give them a hug, and ask their forgiveness because He has new mercies for today!

Broken relationships that have remained shattered for years due to your negligence? Make the call, send the text, get together for coffee because He's giving you new mercies for today!

Failed a test at school? Load your backpack, and get there before the bell rings because He's giving you new mercies for today!

Staring at a bad prognosis and a lifetime of regrets? Pick up the Bible, bow your head, ask for forgiveness and a fresh start because He's giving you new mercies for today!

His love never quits. He won't run out of mercies. He is always there. So lift your chin. Lift your heart. And lift your hands... because He has new mercies for you today!

Scripture To Study: Lamentations 3:19-24
Key Verse: "His mercies begin afresh each morning."
Prayer: *Heavenly Father, I may not have gotten everything right yesterday, but I thank You for this new day and for the new mercies You give me to make me ready for it. Let's do this! I love You, and...*

DAY 80
GET TO THE KING

As we prepared to go visit family for Thanksgiving Day, I introduced the boys to a tradition I grew up with... watching Macy's Thanksgiving Day parade on television. I don't typically pay much attention to the guests coming in to talk with the TV parade hosts, but one of them captured my interest this time. His name is David Oyelowo, a star in the inspirational movie *Queen of Katwe,* the story of a young African girl whose gift for chess inspires her nation.

Oyelowo said, "Chess is a metaphor for life. The goal of chess is to get to the king. Along the way, there will be challenges and trials, but you must do whatever you need to do to get to the king." Of course, he was merely speaking of chess and life in general. But as I watched a parade that I knew would signal the upcoming celebration of the birth of the King of all kings, something inside of me leapt.

The goal 2,000 years ago was to get to the King. Angels made their way to a field outside Bethlehem to announce the birth of the King. Shepherds who heard the good news ran to get to the King. Wise men traveled a great distance for two years to get to the King.

That sparked countless thousands to do all they could to get to the King a little over 30 years later. Some came for healing, or freedom, or advice, but all knew they had to get to the King. In the two millennia which have followed, everyday, across this planet, people still do everything they can to get to the King.

As we approach the kick-off of another Christmas season, let's focus on getting to King. We might get to parades and presents and parties, but may we do our best to get to the King. In the midst of frivolity and chaos, let's set aside time to worship, read His Word, pray, and attend special church services. Let's take David Oyelowo's advice and, "...do whatever you need to do to get to the [King]!"

Scripture To Study: Luke 2:8-20
Key Verse: "They hurried to the village... and there was the baby..."
Prayer: *King Jesus, You are my heart's deepest desire. You have revolutionized my life. I want to be close to You, and I will do whatever I need to in order to get to You. I love You, and...*

DAY 81
MEANWHILE, OFF-STAGE...

I love theater productions. Growing up, my parents took us to broadway-style productions like "Annie Get Your Gun," "Texas," and "Hello, Dolly" at the Moody Outdoor Theater in Galveston. And I loved it!

So, in junior high, I took drama, learning stage makeup, how to not upstage someone, the difference between stage right and stage left. I even starred in in our eighth grade production. In high school, I portrayed the candidate for my opposing political viewpoint in a debate for our school-wide mock election. In college, I found joy in running lights and handling props. I've also enjoyed my fair share of parts in Easter or Christmas productions at churches over the years. But life is not made up of only "on-stage" moments. There are times when we must be "off-stage."

In all the drama stuff I have done over the years, I recall that being off-stage required just as much work as on-stage moments. It takes quiet focus, staying connected with what is happening on-stage, all while changing costumes or grabbing props for myself or others in order to be ready for the next scene in which I will be involved on-stage. Just because people can't see that you are doing something at the moment doesn't mean that you aren't.

King Solomon revealed in the book of Ecclesiastes a truth which the Beatles would thousands of years later make popular... "For everything there is a season, a time for every activity under Heaven." Just because we are not on the stage right now in our life's production, does not mean we are not still part of the cast.

Your next scene is coming up! The director is going to call your name and tell you to get ready to go on. You will once again be in the spotlight where people can see your participation. Serve quietly now, and you will shine brightly later.

Scripture To Study: Ecclesiastes 3:1-8
Key Verse: "... a time for every activity under Heaven."
Prayer: *Dear Lord, please help me to live right when no one is watching just as much as when everyone is watching. Help me to understand and appreciate the behind-the-scenes work You are doing with me as much as the moments in the spotlight. I love You, and...*

DAY 82
BECAUSE I JUST KNOW

Our family *LOVES* going to Silver Dollar City in Branson, MO! One of our boys' favorite areas there is Half Dollar Holler, an area designed for younger kids. And one of their favorite things to do there is to climb through and jump around in the suspended netting of "the treehouse." But it wasn't always Austin's favorite.

Recently, we sat down to watch "old" home videos (from three or four years ago) with the boys. Captured on video was Austin trying to enjoy the treehouse, but it was obvious he was unsure of that netting suspended ten feet above solid earth.

As we watched, Austin told us that he used to be afraid of the bouncing nets of the treehouse because he was afraid he would fall, but he's not afraid now. Sure enough, were you to travel with us to SDC, you'd find him tearing through there with no hesitation whatsoever.

I asked him if he's not afraid anymore because he knows that if it will hold me up, it will definitely hold him up. I was a little shocked when he replied, "No, it's because I've been on it enough times now that I know it will won't let me down." And with that, I sat back in my seat, having been schooled in faith by my six-year old once again. Since it has never let him down before, he has faith that it will never let him down in the future.

In Deuteronomy 31:8, Moses looks Joshua in the eyes and tells him, "*Do not be afraid or discouraged, for the Lord will personally go ahead of you. He will be with you; He will neither fail you nor abandon you.*"

If you're battling a lengthy illness, He won't let you down. If you're dealing with a difficult divorce, He won't let you down. If you're having trouble passing that class at school, He won't let you down. If bills are stacking up higher than paychecks, He won't let you down. He personally goes ahead of you. He *will* be with you.

So go ahead and climb the steep ramp of the treehouse of life. Crawl into the netted area, and jump with confidence alongside Austin. God hasn't let us down before, and He isn't going to this time either.

Scripture To Study: Deuteronomy 31:1-8
Key Verse: "He will neither fail you nor abandon you;"
Prayer: *Father, thank You for being reliable and trustworthy. I depend on You today. I know You will come through for me. I love You, and...*

DAY 83
DOES IT REALLY MATTER?

A few years ago, I went through a three-month fitness and lifestyle transformation program with a group of friends. In one of the training sessions, our coach told us the story of a woman who decided to transform her health one small decision at a time. On average, this woman drank at least nine sodas each day. So her first commitment was to cut out one of those nine sodas per day. After a very short time, she had cut back to only one per day. It was a huge difference for her which began with one small decision.

One day, the Old Testament prophet Elijah visited a woman in the town of Zarephath during the middle of a drought and famine. He asked her to give him something to eat and drink, but she replied that she only had enough to make herself and her son one more meal before they completely ran out and starved to death. In what seems like a cruel request, Elijah asks her to make him some food first. In that moment, this woman made a small decision which impacted her destiny. Because of her decision to honor God by feeding this prophet first, she never ran out of oil or flour from that day till the famine was over.

I once read an old Japanese fable which tells about a jungle which caught on fire. As the fire spread and grew worse, all the animals began to make their way out of the jungle to safety. All except for one lone hummingbird. It would fly to a nearby lake, scoop up a few drops of water in its beak, fly back to fiery jungle and drop the water on the fire. After having passed the crowd of exiting animals several times, one of the elephants asked why the hummingbird was making this futile effort. The hummingbird responded, "I'm doing what I can."

Our decisions determine our destiny. Take that to heart today. Small decisions have power to shape your future. Choose the small kindness. The small generosity. The small courage. The small compliment. Even if it takes some time to show its effects, stick with it. Sometimes our destiny is revealed by our legacy.

Scripture To Study: 1 Kings 17:8-16
Key Verse: "... but make a little bread for me first."
Prayer: *Dear Lord, please help me today to do what I can do and to trust You for what I cannot do. I believe for more. I love You, and...*

DAY 84
TAKE FIVE

Have you ever stood in your closet for much longer than was necessary trying to decide what to wear? Sadly, I have. Have you ever fretted over a bad decision and let it ruin your day? Sadly, I have. Have you ever said something and the moment the words slipped through your lips you immediately wished you had never spoken them? Sadly, I have. Too many times I have let something minor become way bigger in my mind and emotions than I should have.

In Matthew 6, Jesus says we shouldn't let temporary issues cloud what really matters. In fact, He says all our worrying cannot even add a single moment to our lives, and so it is pointless to let a molehill turn into a mountain in our minds.

Here's my recommendation for all of us who struggle to keep life in its proper perspective on occasion... Take five. Ask yourself...

- Will this really matter five minutes from now?
- How about five hours from now?
- Will I be concerned about this five days from now?
- Will this bother me five weeks from now?
- Is anyone at all going to care that this happened five months from now?
- Will I or anyone else even remember this five years from now?
- Will this have had any significant bearing on my life five decades from now?
- And lastly, five hundred years from now, when I have passed on into eternity, will this have made any eternal impact on mine or anyone else's soul forever?

Most of the time, when I practice taking five, I don't get past five hours or five days before I realize that many things I think are such a big deal at the moment are truly trivial. So let's take five today, and get a little perspective... which just might also help us have less, "Sadly, I have's."

Scripture To Study: Matthew 6:19-34
Key Verse: "So don't worry about these things..."
Prayer: *Jesus, please help me keep my life in proper perspective. Help me focus on what is truly important for eternity. I love You, and...*

DAY 85
A REAL HEAD SLAMMER

Our youth pastor, David, was taking a group of us door-to-door, praying with people in the neighborhoods surrounding our church. We dropped off the others while David and I tackled an apartment complex. We pulled in, and David parked the van. I hopped out of the van and slammed the sliding door shut without even looking behind me, but the van door didn't make the normal sound and seemed to not even go all the way closed. "Oh, well," I thought, "I'll just slam it again." And I did. SLAM! Still nothing.

I turned to see what was keeping the door from shutting properly just in time to see David grabbing both sides of his head and falling backward onto the seat. He thought I heard him coming behind me. So his head was just coming through the path of the door as I gave it my first slam. Stunned, David couldn't move. Then... SLAM again!

His head hurt for weeks, and months later certain things still triggered pain in his temples from it. David quickly forgave me, even though I know he had to have been frustrated with me.

In the Old Testament, Joseph faced a few head-slams himself. Thrown into a pit to die and then sold into slavery— by his family nonetheless— falsely accused and thrown into prison, forgotten by a guy he helped. SLAM! SLAM! SLAM!

Then suddenly Joseph's life turns around for the positive as he escalates to second in command of the most powerful nation in the world at that time. In one of the most amazing verses in Scripture, Genesis 45:15 tells us that as Joseph wept with joy, he kissed each of his brothers, and they began talking freely with each other as the relationships were restored.

The truth is, we all get our heads slammed in the van door of life sometimes, but if you will give the pain to God, the pain will stop at some point. He will bring about healing. He will make things right. There might be an occasional wince as your mind recalls the incident, but that will fall away into the joy of being healed from the hurt.

Scripture To Study: Genesis 45:1-15
Key Verse: "Weeping with joy, he embraced...his brothers."
Prayer: *Dear Lord, please heal my hurts. They seem unbearable at the moment. I trust You to take away the pain. I love You, and...*

DAY 86
A LITTLE SOMETHING EXTRA

I don't know the young man or young woman's name who took our order at the counter of the McDonald's on the main strip in Gatlinburg, TN that evening, but I remember the feeling I had walking out of the building and showing PR31 the tallest ice cream cone I had ever received for a buck at any McDonald's.

We were on vacation and splurging for a little treat on a cool October evening. We had walked up and down the strip, enjoying a leisurely time together. I had no idea that I would walk out of that restaurant with ice cream so tall it might topple off the cone if I tilted it too far one way or the other. It was a little something extra to top the night off that ended up making our vacation memorable. What that person did for us that night was kind.

Kindness is when we do a little something extra for someone... whether they deserve it or not, earned it or not, asked for it or not, paid for it or not. It is an attitude of generosity.

In Scripture, King David once asked if there was anyone from Saul's family to whom he could show kindness. It was a rare thing in his day to be kind to your predecessor's family. Plus, Saul was the guy who had tried to hunt him down in order to kill him. Yet David made a choice to be kind to Saul's family because of his friendship with Saul's son, Jonathan, and because he wanted to have a right attitude.

Sound familiar? We live in a world where kindness is a rarity. Some people think it's outdated, but I've never met a person who didn't appreciate it. Everyone wants— and needs— that little something extra... kindness.

So today, let's tip that waitress a little more than we have to. Let's take cookies to a friend, or send someone a text just to let them know they're amazing. Let's spiral the ice cream a little taller on the cone than is expected. Your kindness might just make someone's day.

Scripture To Study: 2 Samuel 9
Key Verse: "I intend to show kindness to you..."
Prayer: *Lord, You are always kind to me. Let me live with that same heart. Help me to pay Your kindness forward to those around me. Impact others through me with kindness. I love You, and...*

DAY 87
PAYBACK TIME

As a young teenager, Saturday nights meant pro-wrestling on TV after everyone went to bed in our house. Midsouth Wrestling no less. Think Junkyard Dog. Hacksaw Jim Duggan. Ted Dibiase. The Von Erichs. The Midnight Express. The Rock-N-Roll Express. It was almost a religious experience for me.

One of the story lines that played out time and again would be a match between a "good guy" and a "bad guy." The good guy would be winning until the bad guy cheated... like pulling brass knuckles from his tights and slamming the unsuspecting good guy. The tide would turn, and now the bad guy had the advantage.

Suddenly, one of the good guy's friends would come racing out of the locker room where he had "seen the incident unfold on closed circuit TV." This friend would slide into the ring to rescue his friend, and it would be payback time. He would physically let the bad guy know he had messed up because the good guy had friends who weren't going to let that abuse go unpunished.

Yes, I know it was fake, that the plots were written out, and those guys knew how to make it appear they were beating each other silly while doing no harm. But in real life, there are times when bad people really do mistreat good people. There are even times when good people mistakenly mistreat other good people. It can even seem the person who did wrong is getting away with it.

However, we have a Friend who is watching it all unfold, and if we will keep a right attitude, heart and spirit, He will rescue us. And when He does, it will be *payback time*! In fact, Zechariah 9 says that God will repay His people double for each trouble inflicted upon them.

So today, if you've been beat down, determine to keep a right attitude, and know that payback time is coming if you'll just leave it to God!

Scripture To Study: Zechariah 9:9-17
Key Verse: "I will repay two blessings for each of your troubles."
Prayer: *Heavenly Father, I trust You are watching. Please be my Defender today, and please help me keep a right spirit so that You can turn my pain into a payback. I love You, and...*

DAY 88
YOU WILL RISE

I'm no cook, but I like food, and I enjoy watching the Food Network. One of my favorite shows recently is *The Pioneer Woman,* starring Ree Drummond. Her culinary expertise is good ol' Southern home cooking. Mmmmmm... just my style. Recently she said something that caught my attention. She was pouring cake batter into a pan to bake and said, "This doesn't look like much in the pan, but it will rise quite a bit in the oven."

Ever felt like that cake batter? Maybe you feel like that right now... like you don't look like much. Those kinds of thoughts come to us all at various times. The key is to remember the second part of what she said. You may not look like much now, but after you've gone through whatever process you're facing at the moment, you're going to rise.

I suppose Timothy, the young pastor in Ephesus, was having to deal with some folks who thought he didn't "look like much in the pan" because his mentor, Paul, wrote him a letter in which he instructed him not to let people look down on him simply because of his age. Instead, he encouraged Timothy to show those folks that he could "rise quite a bit in the oven" and live a life that was far beyond their expectations.

Take that tip from Paul today as if it was written for you... because it was. Ignore those folks who don't think you "look like much in the pan" because of your age, or your gender, or your physical challenge, or your race, or your level of education... or... or... or. Stand up straight. Pull your shoulders back. Look them in the eyes with confidence, and offer a firm handshake. Let them know that you "will rise quite a bit in the oven" by the way you talk to them and behave around them. The way you treat others. The way you pursue God. And the way you are genuine.

You're no ugly cake batter. You, my friend, are a beautiful cake in the baking!

Scripture To Study: 1 Timothy 4
Key Verse: "Don't let anyone think less of you..."
Prayer: *Dear Lord, even though some people may not think much of me, I know You know what I'm made of, and that I will shine for You. Please help me be all I can be for You. I love You, and...*

DAY 89
YOU ARE JUST SUCH A SEED

We homeschool our kids, and recently we began a new year-round model that seems to be working for us. Recently, I've had the opportunity to be at home during the day while they are doing their schooling. Occasionally, on a break from writing, I'll sit in on a lesson or sub for a class if PR31 needs to tackle something else.

The other day, as we were studying science, I read this in Alex's textbook, *"The size of the seed is not determined by the size of the plant... Every seed contains a new living plant."*

I learned that there is a certain palm tree which produces a seed that can weigh as much as fifty pounds! That's more than our son, Austin, weighs! Yet, even though the giant redwood tree is much larger than this palm tree, it produces a significantly smaller seed.

It occurred to me that not only does the size of the plant not determine the size of the seed, but the size of the seed does not determine the size of the plant. That reminded me of Jesus' words in Mark 4 when He said that even though the mustard seed is the smallest of all the seeds, it grows into a large plant where birds can find shelter.

You may view yourself as insignificant. Someone else may seem to have so much more potential. Yet, inside of you, there is everything needed to produce something great, and that something may be much larger than you appear to be as a seed.

You have potential stored up in you. You have greatness in you just waiting to be released. Just like that mustard seed, you have the ability to grow into more and to be a blessing to a lot of others who need what you have to offer.

Let yourself be planted by the Master Gardener. Then sprout, grow, bloom, and produce. Be the seed this world needs! A lot of people around you will be glad you did.

Scripture To Study: Mark 4:30-32
Key Verse: "It is the smallest... but it becomes the largest..."
Prayer: *Jesus, please help me to quit comparing myself to others and simply be who You created me to be. Help me to accomplish all I can for Your Kingdom and glory. I love You, and...*

DAY 90
ROAD TRIP

When I was a child, we would often take these lengthy road trips to visit our extended family. And when I say road trip, I mean like 1,000-1,500 miles one way and 20-24 hours of drive time. We would load everything in the station wagon on a Sunday night after church and hit the road. Mom would drive first, and Dad would sleep. She would get us to daybreak, and then Dad would take the helm to keep us rolling. We stopped only to fuel up and eat. While we rode, we played all the classic road trip games, read, slept, talked... and drove each other nuts.

But you know what? I never thought twice about what direction to drive. Or how much money we would need to take with us. Or whether gas stations were open on Sundays or not. Or when we would arrive. Mom and Dad said, "Get in the car. We're going to see your grandparents." So I did. I just got in that station wagon, and let them do all the planning and driving. They took care of when to stop and when to go. They determined which roads were best for us. They made sure we had all we needed. I just got in and trusted them.

Oh, that I would treat my Heavenly Father the same way. I should just get in the car of life which He is driving, and let Him take care of all the details. Sometimes I do okay. Other times, I'm like a kid trying to tell his parents what time to leave, which road to take, how fast to drive, what time to stop or go. It makes no sense.

In those moments, however, my Heavenly Father is kind and gracious enough to say from Matthew 11:30, "*Keep company with Me, and you'll learn to live freely and lightly.*" (MSG) In other words, "Allen, let me take care of the details. You just get in and ride along with me. I'll get you where you need to be, when you need to be there."

I'm glad He's driving. Since He is, I'm going to climb in the back, relax and have fun looking at the license plates we pass.

Scripture To Study: Matthew 11:28-30
Key Verse: "I will give you rest..."
Prayer: *Heavenly Father, I recognize that You know where to take me and when in life. I choose to let You do the driving, and I'll do the riding. I trust You completely today. I love You, and...*

DAY 91
TRY AGAIN

Brother Hahn, a retired minister from our church, invited us to go fishing with him. Brother Hahn had grandkids, so he had one of those kids' fishing rod-and-reels for me to use. I was in hog heaven, sitting in that boat between my Dad and Brother Hahn, catching bluegills and having the fun I had dreamed of.

I don't remember exactly how it happened, but I somehow lost my grip on the borrowed rod and reel, and down into the water it went. That day, I experienced something which etched in my mind a first memory... *forgiveness*. If Brother Hahn was disappointed or frustrated with me for dropping the rod and reel in the water that day, he never showed it. He told me everything would be alright, and that I shouldn't worry about it. *Forgiveness*.

Months later, Brother Hahn invited us to go fishing again. I was surprised he would let the kid who lost his rod and reel go with him again, but we gratefully accepted the invitation. This day, I experienced another first memory... *grace*. When we arrived, Brother Hahn said, "Here, Allen, you use this one." In his extended hand he held the very rod and reel I had lost on the previous trip. Seems that on a later trip, he had caught the rod and reel I dropped. It was a mess when he caught it, and so he had restored it. Then he invited me to fish with it again. *Grace*.

I was determined not to make the same mistake. I was extra careful this time. It shocked me that he was even willing to let me try again. I could have dropped it again, but he didn't blink.

Brother Hahn was so much like God on both those fishing trips. We make mistakes or just do wrong. Yet in His love and grace, He simply catches what we dropped overboard, cleans it up, hands it back, and says, "Try again."

No matter what you've done or how bad you think it is... no matter how little right you have to be invited once more... try again. This time, maybe hold it a little more carefully... and honor that extended grace by using it well to bring great joy to the heart of the One who shares it with you.

Scripture To Study: Luke 7:36-50
Key Verse: "Then Jesus said... 'Your sins are forgiven.'"
Prayer: *Lord, thank You for Your forgiveness and Your grace. I accept them both humbly today and will live to honor You. I love You, and...*

DAY 92
RENDER THEM SHAMELESS

When I was a teenager, my Dad helped oversee a group of about 25 churches in our fellowship. It was part of his role to help ministers through challenges they might face. One story from a particularly tough year of helping ministers shaped my life...

Late one night our doorbell rang, and Dad informed me that a minister was coming over to talk about something serious. The next morning Dad shared the sad news that this man had made some bad choices which could have cost him his family and his opportunity to minister. To be restored, the man and his wife would have to step away from ministry and attend a different church for a couple of years... our church.

I asked, "Dad, what do I say when I see them Sunday? How am I supposed to treat them?"

I don't think I'll ever forget my Dad's words to me that day. He said, "Well, Allen, they're going to be a part of our church. They're our friends. How do you treat everyone else at our church when you see them?"

I replied, "I say, 'Hi,' smile, and shake their hand or hug them." Dad gently said, "Then that's how you treat these people. They don't have a lot of friends right now. They're already ashamed. They need someone to just love them."

In the months that followed that Sunday when I first smiled at this couple and hugged them, I learned that real love renders people shameless. That's what God does with us... He loves away our shame. 1 John 4:18 tells us that "perfect love expels all fear." That is what shame is, after all... fear that others will realize we don't have it all together. It is fear that people wouldn't accept us if they know "the real us." But love overpowers fear and renders us shameless, allowing us to come back.

Today, let your love prove to others that they don't have to fear. Let your love render them shameless, and watch in amazement as they transform before your very eyes into all they can become.

Scripture To Study: 1 John 4:7-21
Key Verse: "... perfect love expels all fear."
Prayer: *Father, You have given me so much love and grace. Please help me render others shameless by sharing that love. I love You, and...*

DAY 93
NECESSARY

It was taco night at the Chapin house. I was about five years old, and apparently, I was a little too eager for the meal because part way through my taco, I swallowed a bite that I had not chewed well enough. Suddenly, the air stopped flowing into and out of my lungs. A large, triangular piece of taco shell lodged in my throat, and I couldn't breathe. Mom tried to use her finger to dislodge the taco shell, but to no success. They raised my arms and beat on my back, but my face was began turning blue. Fear set in.

Dad turned to my sister Cathy and asked if she had learned that maneuver where you squeeze someone and help free them from choking in her first aid class at school. Cathy said she had, but wasn't sure she knew how to do it without hurting me. Dad told her she had to try because it might be my only hope.

Cathy stood behind me, wrapped her arms around my torso, clasped one hand around the other and suddenly thrust her fist into my diaphragm. Nothing came out. She tried again. Nothing. Mom was crying. Dad was yelling for her to try again. Cathy gave one more big thrust. With that thrust, the triangle-shaped piece of taco shell shot out of my mouth and hurled across the room. I sucked in precious, life-giving air, and the the rest of the family drank in sweet relief.

Cathy may not have enjoyed that class, but none of us cared that night because it paid off. Her willingness to take on the challenge of that class ended up providing her with the very knowledge and skill I needed her to have in order to save my life.

In the same way, God may allow us each to go through some challenging situations in life in order to give us the ability we need to help someone else. So if you're going through a challenging or difficult situation right now in life, don't reject it. It may prove to give you exactly what you need to make a difference in the life of someone else.

Scripture To Study: Romans 5:3-5
Key Verse: "We can rejoice, too, when we run into problems..."
Prayer: *Dear Lord, please help me to view my current challenges as a means of preparing me for future opportunities to serve You and bless others. I love You, and...*

DAY 94
SCARS BEFORE TROPHIES

We were helping our youth pastor build a float to represent our church in a local parade. Someone hurt themselves a little, which led to someone else telling a story of a time when they got hurt. We each took a turn telling a story about getting hurt. Then my friend Mike told an injury story that topped them all. Not to be outdone, we each began pulling out our best injury stories. And after each one of us told our next story, Mike would tell one of his and show us the scar related to that story. As it went on, we all ran out of stories, and Mike just kept telling his till we all laughed harder and harder.

That night, telling stories of injuries we had survived drew us all together. Looking back now, I get it. The most inspiring stories are those which involve someone overcoming adversity. When they show us their scars, they show us their hurt, and they show their healing.

You see, it's not people's successes which inspire us and engage us. It is the scars they show us which they got on the way to winning the trophy. It says to us that, even though we may get hurt, we will heal... and we can even go on to win.

Many people disparage "doubting" Thomas because he refused to believe Jesus had risen from the dead till he saw the scars, but he had not been there when Jesus showed Himself alive the first time. Yet when he saw the scars, it caused him to believe and to be inspired. The scars proved Jesus had overcome!

People still want hope, want to believe, but they need to see some scars. Once they see our scars, they will be able to believe that they, too, can heal from their hurts in life.

So let's pull down our defenses today. Let's be real. Genuine. Authentic. Vulnerable. A little less than perfect. Let's do like Mike, and keep showing our scars till everyone else listening to us thinks, "Hey, my life's not that bad. If they healed up, maybe I will, too." When we do, we will inspire them to believe there is healing and victory for them, too!

Scripture To Study: John 20:24-29
Key Verse: "I won't believe it unless I see the nail wounds..."
Prayer: *Jesus, You were willing to show Your scars. Please help me show mine so that others may believe and be healed. I love You, and...*

DAY 95
AFTER THE CRASH

I was probably in the fourth or fifth grade, and I mounted my metallic electric blue Schwinn with matching banana seat and long, chrome handlebars as my friends and I hit "the shell path," the secret shortcut home to our neighborhood from school. Bryan, Wally, and Scotty were guys I played with almost every day, and we competed a lot. So it wasn't a surprise that, when our bikes hit pavement, we wanted to see who could out-ride each other.

I soon overtook the guys on the short street, navigated the zigzag turn onto the street where Wally and Scotty lived, and broadened my lead. I was so far ahead that, less than a block from my house, I took my hands off the handlebars and looked over my shoulder to see the guys just making the zigzag turn. Then my bike hit a small rock in the road. The long handlebars snapped to the right, causing the bike to stop on a dime, lurch the back end into the air, and hurl me forward with momentous force. I couldn't get my hands in front of me fast enough to keep my chin from hitting the concrete pavement first, and what came next was a blood-curdling scream.

Wally and Scotty heard my scream and never got off their bikes. One of them helped me up and half carried me, the other walked my bike beside us slowly. I was bleeding pretty badly, so they walked me all the way to my front door, rang the doorbell, and waited. When Dad answered the door, they explained what had happened and why I was bleeding so profusely. Dad thanked them for helping me, took me inside and cleaned me up.

I thank God that I had friends who were there to pick me up, help me walk, and carry my load. I want to be that kind of person. I want to hear the cry of someone else in pain, and rush to help them, a friend who will invite the Father to heal their wounds.

Today, we should each strive to be the kind of person who rides to the rescue of fallen friends and helps them— and their beloved bike— home to the Father's loving, healing hands. They will appreciate it... and so will He!

Scripture To Study: Galatians 6:1-3
Key Verse: "Share each other's burdens..."
Prayer: *Lord, please help me to be someone who looks out for the needs of others and helps them in their time of need. I love You, and...*

ALLEN CHAPIN

DAY 96
COME IN FROM THE COLD

It was the coldest weather I've experienced in my entire life. It was minus 40 degrees in the midst of a blizzard which was pounding Moorhead, Minnesota with snow. Mom informed my sister, Karen, and me that it was up to us to go outside, scoop away snow and scrape off ice from the basement windows. I was all of about five or six years old. So at first, this sounded like fun. Then Mom began to bundle me up with warm clothes. "You can only stay out five minutes at most, and then you have to come back inside to warm up," she said.

We trudged outside, found the first window and went to work on it. As soon as we got it cleared off, Karen said we had to go back inside. I gladly obliged her because it was bitterly cold.

When we got inside, we were cold to the bone. Fortunately, Mom had been making hot chocolate. We drank in the heat from the house along with our mugs of steaming hot cocoa. As we finished and I began to relax, she said, "Okay, let's get you suited up so that you can go do the next one."

We repeated this effort several times, and each time it felt like the cold was compounding interest. And each time we came in, Mom was ready to warm us up with something warm.

It's a cold world out there. Blizzard cold. Minus forty cold. People can't stay out in that and survive emotionally or spiritually. They need a place that's warm to thaw out hardened hearts, cynicism, hurts and losses. They need someone in that warm place who has made hot chocolate for the spirit and warm soup for the soul.

Countless times throughout Scripture, God challenges His people to look out for those who have had to endure the coldness of this world... foreigners, widows, orphans, the poor. He wants each of us be the kind of people who say, "Come in from the cold. I'll warm you up. I'll help you get ready to go back out and face what you have to face." Who can you warm up today so they can face the cold again?

Scripture To Study: Isaiah 58:6-12
Key Verse: "Feed the hungry and help those in trouble."
Prayer: *Dear Lord, please help me to see the needs around me which I can meet, and help me to meet them to honor You. I love You, and...*

THE UPSIDE

DAY 97
LOST AND GAINED

Like any decent parent who loves their kids and wants to see them happy, I have at times been the old softy who, after admittedly being a little frustrated, has bought a replacement balloon— or possibly two— to replace one that has floated off into the great unknown. The same is true when ice cream has been dropped on the concrete, or a brand new toy broken the first day. This is especially true if the boys have saved up and spent their own money on something.

Maybe your parents never did that. Maybe you've never done that as a parent. Maybe the philosophy you have lived under, or lived by, was "Tough luck, Chuck. Maybe this will teach you, and maybe next time you won't...".

If so, I'm sorry. I'm sorry because that probably influences the way in which you view God. It is entirely possible that you may think because you sinned... because you blew it... or messed up something... or lost something... you are bad, and you need to learn to be good.

Understand this, though... God is a good, loving and gracious Father. Scripture says that He is slow to get angry and quick to forgive. It says that He delights in bringing joy into our lives.

No matter what stage of life you're in, we all evaluate our lives when we've lost something. Maybe you've lost your health. Or a person you love. Or a job. Or a dream. Whatever the situation, God sees that you lost it. He knows how much you enjoyed it, and He wants to give you something else in its place which will bring you just as much, if not more, joy!

So you made a mistake. Let Him wipe those tears away. And don't be afraid to ask Him to give you something else wonderful in place of what is lost. It's in His heart to do it already. You'll see.

Scripture To Study: Psalm 145
Key Verse: "The Lord is merciful and compassionate..."
Prayer: *Father, thank You for Your mercy, compassion, love, grace and forgiveness. Thank You for restoring joy to me when I experience loss. Please replace what is lost in my life. I love You, and...*

DAY 98
WITH YOU

I have a lot of friends and family facing challenging situations right now. These are situations I would not want to go through personally. These are difficult times for them, and my heart goes out to them. If I were to tell you their individual stories, you would understand.

If I were to guess, I would say you probably understand all too well. Each of us faces the challenges and difficulties caused by living in this world wrecked by the damaging effects of sin. Each of us has dealt with hurt. Loss. Fear. Stress.

One of the most comforting truths we can hold onto when we go through difficult times is that God promises to be *with us*. The reason He said people in Scripture could find strength and confidence to face their challenges was not that the challenges would go away, but that... get this... He would be *with them*.

Joshua leading the Israelites to conquer the Promised Land. Gideon protecting his nation from invaders. Jesus on the boat... in the storm... *with* the disciples. The key was that He was *with them*. When God sent His only Son to this earth, He was called Immanuel... God *with us*. When Jesus was getting ready to ascend back into Heaven some 33 years later, He told His followers they could be bold because He would be *with them* to the end of the age.

The way that you and I can have the courage, the confidence, the patience, the endurance, the compassion, the grace, the strength we need to make it through the difficulties we face in life, is to know deep down that He is indeed *with us*.

He is, you know... *with us*. *With you*.... right now... right here. Find strength and confidence in that today. You are not alone. You are going to make it. He is... *with you*!

Scripture To Study: Joshua 1:1-9
Key Verse: "For the Lord your God is with you wherever you go."
Prayer: *Lord, thank You for constantly being with me. It is so great to know I don't have to face this life alone. With You beside me, I have the courage to keep on and win. I love You, and...*

DAY 99
PURSUED

Today marks two years since we welcomed our pet Schnauzer, Sugar, into the family. The boys had prayed for at least weeks, and probably more like months for the Lord to give us a dog. Then, while we were on a trip to visit my parents, the boys and I "stumbled across her" at a pet adoption day in a local pet store there.

Sugar wasn't much to behold that day. Scraggly, not entirely clean, trapped in that kennel, but that didn't stop us from adopting her. Today, she is clean, regularly bathed and sensibly groomed (albeit not professionally, but pretty dog-gone good). She never runs out of food or water. She has her own kennel now, with her own bed, and her own plethora of toys with which to play. Plus, she has a fenced-in yard. On top of that, she doesn't have to wait for the humans to take notice that she needs to take care of business... she even has a doggie door and can go outside as her heart desires.

I've got to admit, this dog has it made. And so does Sugar. You see, I too, was once pursued and brought into a family. I didn't look like much when God found me. But He cleaned me up and keeps me clean. He provides for me and protects me. I am free to live a life full of joy and peace within the wonderful boundaries He has set out for me... boundaries which keep me near Him. It really is a great life.

I love the quote from Dick Foth in his book, *Known*, "Pursuit affirms value." It reminds me of the three stories Jesus told in Luke 15 about the lost coin, the lost sheep and the lost son. The pursuit of those in each story point to how God pursues us. And it is that very pursuit which declares about each of us that we are of value to Someone... the most important Someone in the Universe.

It's nice to be wanted. Wanted means we have value. You do. You have value. You *are* valuable! Don't forget that today.

Scripture To Study: Luke 15
Key Verse: "Won't he... go and search for the one...?
Prayer: *Heavenly Father, thank You for searching for me until You found me. Thank You for providing for me and protecting me. Thank You for loving me and blessing me. I love You, and...*

DAY 100
MAKE YOUR OWN DOZEN

I pulled the eggs out of the plastic sack to put them in the fridge. They caught my attention because they were a different brand in different packaging. So, to satisfy my curiosity, I asked Angela, "Why the different eggs?" She knows I love a good story, and so she told me how she had come to buy this brand...

She started to get the normal brand, but when she opened the lid to check them, a couple eggs were cracked. She picked up another package and found cracked eggs in it also. Each one she picked up had a cracked egg in it. So, she bought the other brand of eggs instead.

As she finished the story, she said, "Oh, my word! It just hit me. All I had to do to get the eggs I wanted was to swap out the cracked eggs in one carton for un-cracked eggs in another dozen, and I could have had the ones I wanted." The realization made us both laugh. It was a simple solution that just didn't come to mind that day.

Now this was obviously not a crisis in life. Yet each of us face challenging situations which we approach with the same thought process PR31 used in buying eggs that day. We think, "Well, everything I try is messed up. I guess I won't get what I want. I suppose I'll just have to settle for something less." We end up disappointed with life because we think our choices are limited.

But we serve an unlimited God who can think outside the egg carton. James, Jesus' half-brother, wrote in the first chapter of his letter to believers that when we lack wisdom, all we have to do is ask our unlimited God. And He goes on to say that God will gladly, generously help us to think outside the egg carton, too!

Why not do today what James suggested and ask God for wisdom that goes beyond your own natural abilities? It couldn't hurt. It could only help. Go ahead, give it a try. You might just get the kind of eggs you really want!

Scripture To Study: James 1:2-8
Key Verse: "If you need wisdom, ask our generous God..."
Prayer: *Dear Lord, I need Your help. I can't seem to figure my situation out, and I need wisdom. Please guide me. Give me special insight and understanding as I honor You. I love You, and...*

DAY 101
CHEERING AND CHALLENGING

I am officially a fan of the television show *American Ninja Warrior*. I am mesmerized by the level of competition, by how hard these people train, and by the unbelievable feats they make their bodies accomplish. Then there are their back stories. Some of these people have overcome extreme life situations to compete at this level.

What I love most is the way they both challenge *and* cheer for each other at the same time. Each athlete goes out there trying to not only do their own personal best, but to out-do every other athlete competing. They *are* competing to win.

Yet there is no smack-talk between competitors. It's often difficult to determine whether they want to win more themselves, or want one of their competitors to win. While waiting to make their attempt at a course, or having made their attempt— successfully or unsuccessfully— they stand on the sidelines cheering on the very competitors trying to beat them... giving advice... and telling them how much time they have left. When a competitor succeeds, they roar with excitement, jump up and down, high-five them and hug each other. When a competitor fails, they groan and hug them, speaking words of encouragement about how far they got and how they will succeed the next time.

The Apostle Paul challenged the believers at Philippi to cheer each other on like this... to encourage each other as they each strove to do the best they could in living lives that honored Christ.

We can do that. We *should* do that. We should each press to do the best we can, and we should also cheer for those competing alongside us. This is not something restricted to *American Ninja Warriors*. It is a culture they have created. And we can create it where we live, work, serve, and shop... *if* we want to. I want to. Will you join me?

Scripture To Study: Philippians 2:1-4
Key Verse: "...working together with one mind and purpose."
Prayer: *Lord, please help me to not only do my best for You, but to encourage others to do their best. May we honor You and all You've done for us by living like You. I love You, and...*

DAY 102
WORTH THE CLIMB

As we walked down the hill at Almagor, overlooking the Sea of Galilee in Israel, back to the waiting tour bus, Michaela was unusually quiet. When I asked if she was okay, she began to open up...

She told how she had not prepared enough physically for the trip, and she wasn't sure she would even be able to make the climb up the hill when we started our trek. Several had to encourage her to keep climbing. In truth, she almost gave up. But at that moment when she considered going back to the bus, she felt like the tour guide wouldn't be bringing her up there if it wasn't worth it. Plus, she didn't want to miss out on anything after having paid all that money and traveled all that way. So she climbed.

Then the tears began to flow from her eyes as the words flowed from her mouth. She told how, after the teaching we had heard... when we had time to stand and overlook the area where more than 90% of what was recorded about Jesus' earthly ministry took place, she was so glad she had not given up, but had kept climbing. She thought of how Jesus Himself had climbed this hill, seen this landscape, and talked with His Father. That's when the Lord spoke quietly and gently to her heart, telling her that if she would always climb the challenging mountains of life, He would climb with her, always making sure the climb was worth it.

Today, you may have a challenging mountain in front of you, and you don't feel like you can keep going on. You may feel like you weren't prepared for it. You may feel like you don't have what it takes. You may wonder if the climb is worth the effort.

Keep climbing. You can make it to the top. Make God your climbing partner. Let Him lead you to heights you have not scaled before, because He has sights to show you, and truths to reveal to you, and blessings to give you. And when you get to the top, the view will be amazing. Make the climb. Don't give up. It *is* going to be worth it!

Scripture To Study: John 6:1-13
Key Verse: "Then Jesus climbed a hill and sat down with His disciples around Him."
Prayer: *Jesus, I want to climb every hill with You. Please give me strength, and remind me of what awaits me at the top. I love You, and...*

DAY 103
FLASHY VS. FAITHFUL

For those of us who love the game, we want to watch football players *play* the game. Most of us are not interested in watching them practice. Or sit in team meetings. Or work out. Or do the physical therapy. Or eat their meals. Or buy groceries. Or just the routine of life. And after their glory days in the game are over, most of them are forgotten. It's because our society as a whole does not value faithfulness.

We want quick. We want big. We want flashy. But we typically underrate faithfulness. Yet faithfulness is what we want in a spouse. Or friends. Or work. I wonder what would happen if we began to applaud faithfulness. Celebrated it over razzle-dazzle.

Scripture points out that "...your faithful service is an offering to God." Faithful service. Imagine that. It might sound normal, plain, and boring, but God says every time you make the kids a meal, or mow the grass, or pray for someone who is sick, or go to work— if you have the right attitude about it— you are giving God an offering. You don't even have to open your wallet.

So let's celebrate the teacher who has been teaching for twenty years, and commits to ten more. Let's celebrate the couples who are faithfully committed in marriage, and are committed for a lifetime. Let's celebrate the pastor of that small, rural church who has visited hospitals, performed funerals, and taken food to the homebound. Let's celebrate the nurse who dispenses medicines, gives sponge baths, empties bedpans, checks vitals and assists doctors with no fanfare.

Jesus said in Matthew 25 that if we do exactly what we're talking about here, one day we will meet the Lord face-to-face, and He will celebrate us as "good and faithful servants." The "good" part is the goodness *He* gives us with salvation. The "faithful" part is what *we* do with that goodness. That's what we can do that He will celebrate. So, let's choose to be faithful, not just flashy... and one day it will be celebrated!

Scripture To Study: Matthew 25:1-30
Key Verse: "Well, done... You have been faithful..."
Prayer: *Father, I am so grateful for Your goodness imparted to me through Jesus. I want to honor Your goodness to me with my faithfulness to You. Help me keep on. I love You, and...*

DAY 104
WRONG PLACE, RIGHT TIME

As I walked across the parking lot and started to get into my vehicle after having preached the Sunday morning service at a church in Texas recently, I noticed these little flowers growing in the midst of nothing but rocks. No grass. No other plants. They looked so out of place, but there they were, just growing and beaming brightly. They brightened my day because they reminded me that God can cause us to flourish regardless of our situation.

I'm reminded of Isaiah 35 as I think of them today. It is a chapter of hope. It speaks of how God can bless when and where He chooses, regardless of how bleak the situation appears.

Today, you may be going through a difficult time. Perhaps your health is under attack, like a couple friends of ours are right now. Or maybe you're facing some financial challenges that have your back against a wall like another person I know. Or maybe you're going through a drought in the area of friendships.

Know this... God doesn't need your situation to be perfect. Or optimal. Or favorable. Or even okay... to cause your life to blossom right now! He can cause life to spring out of death. He can cause health to spring out of sickness. He can cause abundance to spring out of lack. He can cause companionship to spring out of loneliness.

What looks impossible to you is completely and easily possible with Him. You may think you're in the wrong place, but don't worry because at the right time God can cause your life to push up through those desert rocks and bud... and bloom... and blossom into fullness!

Why not take some time to look up the 35th chapter of Isaiah today, and find some encouragement there? That chapter is full of the kind of hope I've found in knowing Christ personally and following Him. I believe that if you'll open your heart today, you'll find that same hope... and bloom among the rocks!

Scripture To Study: Isaiah 35
Key Verse: "The wasteland will rejoice and blossom..."
Prayer: *Dear Lord, life looks pretty bleak right now. My situation seems to have no possible improvement. Please, work a miracle and bring something out of nothing. I love You, and...*

DAY 105
BETTER DAYS AHEAD

When I was in college, my dad was selected to help lead the nearly 300 churches of our denomination in the area of Texas where we lived. He succeeded the Rev. J. B. Linney, a Godly gentleman who had served in that role with excellence for a number of years. Bro. Linney had a saying he always used, regardless of the situation. When he retired, he used it in his closing address to the ministers gathered at that meeting. His statement was this... *"There are better days ahead!"*

Now that makes sense if we're facing tough times, but it doesn't instantly make sense if times are great. When we feel well-compensated, healthy and loved, who thinks about "better?" J. B. Linney, that's who. Bro. Linney understood that God is not limited to the good things we enjoy right now, but He has even greater blessings of all kinds waiting on us.

I hear people say high school was the best time of their life. Or that their best years were their college years. Or that the day they got married was the greatest day of their life. That's a little sad to me. It's as if they have given up hope for the future being better than the past.

Don't get me wrong. I am grateful beyond words for the generosity of the Lord in blessing me to this point in life, but I'm with J. B. Linney... "There are better days ahead!" No matter how tough, or how terrific, life is... There are better days ahead! And when I breathe my last breath on this planet, guess what... there will still be better days ahead for me, as I get to spend the rest of eternity even closer to Jesus!

Your best days are still ahead of you, too, if you commit them to the Lord. Choose today to enjoy good memories of the past, but to also realize there is so much more to look forward to. Today is going to be better than yesterday, and tomorrow will top today. Thanks for the life lesson, Bro. Linney! I'm with you!!!

Scripture To Study: I Corinthians 2:1-6
Key Verse: "... no mind has imagined what God has prepared for those who love Him."
Prayer: *Heavenly Father, I believe You have better prepared for me than I have now or can imagine. I receive it today. I love You, and...*

DAY 106
BOLD PREDICTIONS

I love watching NFL football. It's kind of like how PR31 feels when the *Countdown To Christmas* starts on Hallmark Channel, and they start showing the Christmas romantic comedy movies every day.

Additionally, when I'm traveling by myself, I enjoy listening to the NFL Network on satellite radio. One of those shows allows fans to call in late during each week and make bold predictions about how they think their team will fare in the upcoming week's games. The only guidelines are that you have to predict that your team will win, and give a legitimate reason as to why in the form of a bold prediction. Some callers say their team will win by a resounding score because their defense will score three times, or because their quarterback will throw four touchdown passes. It's both entertaining and inspiring.

We Christians ought to live that way, too. We ought to make bold predictions about our lives. Truth is, we actually have a solid foundation on which to base these bold predictions... the Word of God. God *always* keeps His promises and *never* fails. So, we can make bold predictions when we line our lives up with Him.

We can make bold predictions like:
- *By His stripes we are healed. (Isaiah 53:5)*
- *No good thing will He withhold from those who live uprightly. (Psalm 84:11)*
- *God will supply all your needs. (Philippians 4:19)*
- *God knows the plans He has to prosper us and not to harm us. (Jeremiah 29:11)*
- *We will lie down in peace and sleep. (Psalm 4:8)*
- *He will never leave us nor forsake us. (Deuteronomy 31:6)*
- *He will repay two blessings for each of our troubles. (Zechariah 9:12)*

Begin today to speak those bold predictions over yourself, your family and your friends. If people can call in and make random guesses about a football game, we followers of the eternal God can definitely make bold predictions rooted in proven truth!

Scripture To Study: Deuteronomy 7:7-11
Key Verse: "He is the faithful God who keeps His covenant..."
Prayer: *Lord, thank You for making promises to me. I accept them today and believe You will keep them. I love You, and...*

DAY 107
CHECK MARKS ARE COMING

Alex and Austin have faith. How do I know? They have these prayer journals, and in them they write or draw a picture of things they are asking God to do for them. They have prayed we would get a dog, and also for things like video games they want. Those are cute, but recently they added a close family friend who has been battling some serious health issues. They love this person, and have been believing God would heal them. It has been so great to hear their whispered prayers under our out-loud prayers each night. Their faith inspires me.

When a prayer in their book gets answered by God, they put a check mark on that page, showing them that God did what they asked of Him. When there is something they want or need, they put it in their prayer book because every request in there has a check mark by it. Every... last... one. In their mind, they simply ask God to help them out, believe Him, and wait for it to happen. When something isn't happening in their desired time frame, they don't quit believing just because it hasn't happened yet. Instead, they simply flip through the previous pages and see all the check marks, remembering that God always comes through for them. Imagine that.

We adults can have prayer books, too, and we can trust God to come through for us. Go back through your life, and look at all the check marks already placed beside so many things He has done for you. Then don't give up believing for those pages that haven't gotten their check marks... YET.

For the record, since we prayed for that friend, their health has turned around completely to the amazement of the doctors... but not to Alex and Austin. They just believed the God who gave our family a dog, and them the video game they wanted, could just as easily heal our friend. It was no surprise to them because... check marks are coming!

Scripture To Study: Matthew 18:1-4
Key Verse: "...become like little children..."
Prayer: *Jesus, I'm sorry for those times I have doubted in the past. Beginning today, I choose to believe that You will always come through for me. I love You, and...*

DAY 108
MISTLETOE MOMENTS

There is something wonderful about a kiss. I mean a real, genuine, non-hyper-sexualized kiss... an authentic, sweet, tender kiss. It's a wonderful gift to both the kiss-er and the kiss-ee.

At Christmas time, when we see mistletoe, we almost always think of a kiss. I don't see mistletoe everywhere I go. It seems like a rare trimming these days. (Maybe we just have a lot more Spanish moss in Louisiana.) But I don't even see a lot of fake mistletoe. You'd think junior high boys would buy it by the truckloads on Amazon and hang it all over the city... you know, just in case. But sadly, it's a rare sight.

Too bad, because when I think of mistletoe and a genuine kiss, I think of how Scripture tells us that the virgin would conceive a son who would be, "Immanuel, which means, 'God is with us.'"

"God with us," think of it! He chose to not be a distant Deity, disconnected from the realities of our lives. Instead, like the song says, "Heaven meets earth like an unforeseen kiss." Mistletoe.

God came near, came close. Close enough to hear our heart beat. Close enough to feel our breath on His face. And it didn't matter to Him that our hearts weren't right or that our breath stunk. He just wanted to be with us.

So He came. He stood under the mistletoe at just the right time and came near us. He kissed us with His presence for 33 years, and we have never forgotten that kiss. Two thousand plus years later, and we still remember the night God slipped into human flesh to be with us.

Mistletoe. It's the Christmas trimming that reminds me most of God's desire for a pure, intimate, close, gentle, tender relationship with me... and with you. So the next time you see some mistletoe, take a moment to pause and soak in His Immanuel presence. He'll meet you right there. And Christmas will be more special than ever.

Scripture To Study: Matthew 1:18-25
Key Verse: "...Immanuel, which means 'God is with us.'"
Prayer: *Father, thank You for choosing to be with us, and thank You for pulling us close to You. I am so glad You are close enough to hear me whisper. I love You, and...*

DAY 109
WARM LIGHTS

Where our house is situated, there are a lot of trees and very few street lights. Since our house sits back off the road, it's quite dark at night. When we know we'll be getting home at night, we normally turn on some outside lights and then use the light from our phones to get from the carport to front door of the house.

At Christmas time, though, it's quite a different story. Lining the edge of the roof along the front of our house are strands of multi-color, C-9 size Christmas lights. Add to that the glow from other lighted Christmas decorations, and you can see everything clearly. I could park without using headlights when they are all lit up. As long as the lights are up and illuminated, there is a sense of safety and warmth.

It's easy to read about Jesus coming to this earth as a baby and think the world He was born into was a more morally upright, easier world to live in than ours, but that would be a misconception. The world Jesus was born into was full of hyper-sexuality, substance abuse, world powers using brutality, bribes, and political deals done in the dark of night. At both the beginning and the end of His life here on earth, leaders were trying to kill Jesus to save their own power. The world at Christ's birth was every bit as dark as ours is today.

It's precisely because the world was so dark that God sent His only Son to be a light. John 1:5 says, "The light shines in the darkness, and the darkness can never extinguish it."

Light always wins, and since Jesus is the light of the world, then we can rest assure that— though things may look dark around us— that darkness cannot overcome us because we have the light of the world living in us.

So, every time you see those Christmas lights this season, remember... no matter how bad things look right now, if you invite Jesus into the situation, He always drives the darkness away!

Scripture To Study: John 1:1-9
Key Verse: "The light shines in darkness..."
Prayer: *Lord, thank You for coming into this world and dispelling darkness for us. Warm my heart today with Your light. I love You, and...*

DAY 110
CRAZY LIGHTS

Growing up, we lived in a neighborhood in which the homeowners association required every house to be decorated for Christmas no later than the first Saturday in December. People from all around drove through our streets, ooh-ing and ahh-ing. Some people like us had normal displays, but others hired professionals to make their houses stand out. I always loved seeing those houses. Those people knew what it meant to go big!

I can't help but laugh (and cheer) while watching the 2006 Christmas movie, *Deck The Halls*. Neighbors played by Danny Devito and Matthew Broderick compete to see which one can outdo the other to have the brightest, most elaborate light display at their house for Christmas. I love even more that Danny Devito's character has this life-long goal of his house being so lit up for Christmas that it can be seen from space.

I don't know what your thing is. Maybe it's hanging Christmas lights to delight kids. Or perhaps writing songs that are sung in churches around the world every Sunday. Or maybe even raising great kids who grow up to positively impact the lives of everyone around them. Whatever it is, GO BIG! Don't be mediocre. Don't play it safe. Don't hedge your bets. Throw yourself into it whole hog!

God designed us to be enthusiastic. Without getting too deep, the word enthusiasm comes from a Greek thought which means filled with God. Inside your body is a creative being, made in the image of God, with all the ability you need to go big. In reality, to go big is to live like God.

So cook a feast big enough to feed an army. Run your personal best in a marathon! Run for office, and lead with integrity. Or run a corporation based on godly principles that makes a difference in this world. Be the best baker, or CPA, or computer specialist, or high school coach you can be. Be the best parent or foster parent you can be. Just make sure that whatever you do, you do it with enthusiasm!

Scripture To Study: Ephesians 6:7
Key Verse: "Work with enthusiasm..."
Prayer: *Dear Lord, fill me full of Your Spirit of creativity and passion today so that I can live to honor You. I love You, and...*

THE UPSIDE

DAY 111
THE MEAL

One of my favorite parts of celebrating Christmas is the Christmas meal! Yum!!! Who doesn't love a great Christmas meal?

What is it about the Christmas meal that is so different? It's not like I never eat turkey or ham at any other time of the year. I'm not passing up the potato salad at the Fourth of July. And since I feel like a meal is not complete without dessert, I eat cookies, cake, or pie on multiple occasions throughout the year. Is it that we've gotten together to eat with family or friends whom we rarely get to see? Or is it the decorations and the way in which the table is set, whether you pull out the fine china or use those really fancy paper plates?

I'll tell you what it is. *Abundance.* The amount of food at the meal stands out to me. It is the bookend of massive meals on the other side of a massive holiday season from Thanksgiving. I cannot remember a Christmas meal in my lifetime where there was not way more food than necessary for the number of people present. Leftovers are not accidental at this meal. They are intentional. Am I scared that there won't be any left when I go back for seconds... or thirds? No way! There is an abundance.

When I think about the Christmas meal, it reminds me that the God who lavishly and generously gave His Son to win our hearts and souls for eternity is a God of abundance. His grace, love, and provision never run out. In fact, Paul reminds us in Ephesians 3:20 that God is able to do, "...infinitely more than we might ask or think." He is the God of more than enough. The God of abundance. We can't out-ask Him. He has prepared more than enough for us. It is reassuring and comforting to know He will never run out.

So, as you (over)fill your plate this Christmas with delicious delicacies which delight your tastebuds as part of celebrating God giving His only Son, remember that He still has more waiting for you... and He will never run out. Even if you go back for seconds!

Scripture To Study: Ephesians 3:14-21
Key Verse: "...His glorious, unlimited resources..."
Prayer: *Father, I am glad that You are unlimited, full of abundance and generosity toward me. Fill me full today. I love You, and...*

115

DAY 112
A HIPPO?

Each year it seems that a different Christmas song resonates within my heart for the season. Most of the time, it's a very touching, spiritual song with some deep truth which speaks to the very core of my soul.

This past Christmas was no different... sort of. The song that drilled so deeply into my heart last Christmas was... wait for it... "I Want A Hippopotamus For Christmas" performed by Gayla Peevey! It touched me somewhere deep down inside, and I just couldn't stop listening to it. Literally, I don't think I can count how many times I listened to it that Christmas. It got way down deep in my soul.

The power of the song goes far beyond the hypnotic grasp of the young lady's odd voice as she belts it out. There is something about the song that challenges my faith. I mean, really, who asks for a hippo for Christmas and won't let up?

That's crazy. That's crazy faith. I mean, that's as crazy as believing that a perfect God would send His perfect Son to come to earth as a baby... let that Son grow up to live a perfect life... and then let cruel people execute His perfect Son to pay for my crimes against this perfect God. Seriously, who would believe that? Me!

And if I'll believe Him for something so outrageous as that, what makes me think that He wouldn't listen when I believe in His love and ask Him for something far simpler?

Or maybe a better question is... Why are we not willing to ask God for outrageous blessings when He has already proven His love so deeply? He's not holding out on us. He *wants* to bless us. When our hearts beat in sync with His, I don't believe there is anything we could ask for that He wouldn't give!

So let's get crazy with our faith today and every day. Let's just go ahead and ask. Let's ask big. We can't surprise or out-do Him... even with a hippo!

Scripture To Study: John 16:23-28
Key Verse: "Ask using My name, and you will receive..."
Prayer: *Jesus, help me to have a fuller understanding today of how deeply our Father wants to bless me. Give me big faith to ask big. I love You, and...*

DAY 113
THE TREE

I love a Christmas tree! Real or artificial. Single-color lights or multi-color lights. Burlap or ribbon. Garland or popcorn strands. Icicles or faux snow. Star or angel on top. I love a Christmas tree. When I see a Christmas tree, I usually don't think of stores or gifts. Well, maybe one gift. I think of another tree, one that came at the end of Christ's life... the Cross. You see, when the decorations are removed and the needles have fallen off a real Christmas tree, what's left is wood, a center vertical post with horizontal branches... a Cross.

The Cross really is why Jesus came to earth. Yes, He loved people, taught people, and healed people. Yes, He brought truth and stood against injustice. But in the end, He came not only to live, but to die so that we who were separated from God could be made right with God.

I know it's difficult to think about His suffering and death on our behalf when we are caught up in the magic of Christmas and the mystery of God arriving as a baby. The warm lights and soft music of Christmas seem to shield us from the harshness of how He would be treated because of us, but it is reality none-theless. And honestly, I'm happy that He was willing to take my place and my punishment. I am not good enough to match God's standard of goodness. I needed a Savior, and so God in His great love sent one... His own Son!

So, when I see a Christmas tree, I celebrate a little more... because I once was lost and now I'm found. I was once a sinner and now I'm a son of God. And it's all because of a tree... The Cross.

You can debate and get frustrated over the hoopla some folks generate about Christmas trees if you want to. But as for me and my house, we choose to let ours serve as a reminder of our Savior!

Scripture To Study: Matthew 1:18-25
Key Verse: "...name Him Jesus, for He will save His people from their sins."
Prayer: *Jesus, thank You for coming to not only to live, but to die in my place. I celebrate Your gift of eternal life to me. No one and nothing in all of life could be as special to me as You. I love You, and...*

DAY 114
PRAY BOLD PRAYERS

With wind blowing and sleet falling, our Israeli tour guide, Ilan, told how Joshua had stood in the area we were standing and prayed a bold prayer, asking God to make the sun and moon stand still so he could defeat the enemy whom the Israelites were battling.

Ilan told us how other groups had prayed a bold prayer in the same place Joshua had prayed and how miracles had taken place. Then he said, "Pastor Allen, lead us in a bold prayer."

Me? A prayer like Joshua? I was nervous, but I asked people to share their bold requests. Jokingly, one guy added at the end, "Could we pray that it would stop sleeting on us?" We all laughed at this request, and then we prayed.

Concluding I said, "And Lord, please make it stop sleeting so that we can see the wonderful sites today in order that we could grow closer to You. Amen!" We opened our eyes, and the sleet immediately stopped, the clouds parted, and the sun shone through over the exact spot in Jerusalem where we were headed next. Our jaws dropped. We looked at each other and just laughed. The God who had stopped the sun and moon for Joshua had just answered *our* bold prayer, despite its simplicity. Suddenly we were aware that He could answer the other bold prayers we had just prayed.

For the rest of the trip, anytime we had a challenge, someone would say, "Pray a bold prayer." Once, we even prayed for the wi-fi on the bus to start working again so that we could communicate with our loved ones back home, and before we said "amen," we were connected.

The God who stopped the sun in its tracks, stopped the sleet for sightseers, and made the wi-fi work for loved ones is still exceedingly abundantly able to do more than we could ever ask, think or imagine!

What bold prayer do you need to pray today? Forget how small your faith is. Consider how big God is. Pray a bold prayer!

Scripture To Study: Joshua 10:12-14
Key Verse: "There has never been a day like this one before or since..."
Prayer: *Dear Lord, since You can handle anything, I am bringing You my bold prayer today and believing You to come through for me. No one else can do this for me. I trust You. I love You, and...*

DAY 115
CHECK YOUR CITIZENSHIP

I voted. Not that I felt like most of the candidates fit my worldview. I certainly don't attest to the integrity of most. But I voted because it is my privilege as a citizen of this nation.

I'm not just a citizen of this country in which I live physically, though. Isaiah prophesied about Jesus Christ that He would be called the "Prince of Peace." Since He is a Prince, then we know that His Father must be the King of Peace. And since there is a King of Peace, then there must be a Kingdom of Peace.

Now, when a person chooses to make God the King of their life, then they become a citizen of His Kingdom... the Kingdom of Peace. That makes all Christians citizens of Peace, the place where they dwell.

The Apostle Paul writes in Philippians 4:7 that, as citizens of God's Kingdom, we "will experience God's peace, which exceeds anything we can understand. His peace will guard your hearts and minds as you live in Christ Jesus." A place where the King exceeds my expectations and the Prince protects me sounds like the place I belong.

My freedom to vote in this country was bought by others who put their lives on the line for me to have that right in the place where I live, and my right to live in the Kingdom of Peace was bought by the Prince who put His life on the line to offer me citizenship. When I voted today, I affirmed and celebrated my citizenship of my country. And when I choose to live in peace, I affirm and celebrate my citizenship in God's Kingdom.

If you are not experiencing peace in your life right now, renew your citizenship in God's Kingdom. The only ID you will need to show is that you have accepted His Son, the Prince of Peace... Jesus. Peace, it's a great place to live!

Scripture To Study: Philippians 4:6-7
Key Verse: "His peace will guard your hearts and minds as you live in Christ Jesus."
Prayer: *Father, thank You for granting me citizenship in Your Kingdom of Peace. I accept that citizenship with all its blessings. I choose not to worry, but to give my concerns to You today. I love You, and...*

DAY 116
MISSING PIECES

The boys and I have this 1,000-piece puzzle featuring a photo of a New Orleans Saints football game in the Superdome. It's ridiculous. I'm not even sure we have found all the edge pieces inside the box yet. We work on it for awhile, and we set it aside because something is missing that we just can't find, but I guarantee you that when we get down to the last few pieces, we won't be stopping till we complete it. We won't leave that last missing piece out.

Likewise, when something important is missing in our lives, it becomes the sole focus, taking up all our extra attention, energy, and time trying to find that last piece which we think will complete us. When you're depressed, it takes everything you've got to try to find the missing joy. When you're stressed about a situation you're facing, it takes almost all your energy to try find peace. Missing pieces can drive you crazy trying to find them.

God knows what it is to be laser-focused on something, or someone, missing. Jesus illustrated just how focused God is on what's missing in the three stories He told in Luke chapter 15. It's one of my favorite chapters in all of Scripture because it reminds me that God goes looking for what is lost, and He doesn't stop until He finds it.

What's missing in your life today? Are you missing a job that you would love? Are you missing health? Are you missing money in the bank? Are you missing true, authentic friends? Are you missing genuine understanding and solutions?

Whatever you're missing today, God cares deeply about it. He cares deeply about you! He cares so much that He is willing to go to great lengths to find what's missing in your life and fill that void. So if you're missing direction, wisdom, love, provision, or anything else... bring your emptiness to Him and He will find your missing pieces!

Scripture To Study: Luke 15
Key Verse: "Rejoice with me because I have found my lost sheep."
Prayer: *Dear Lord, I have so much in life, and yet I am missing this one thing. It seems to absorb all my energy trying to get it. Please help bring completeness my life as only You can. I love You, and...*

DAY 117
KEEP TRUSTING

As I mowed a couple acres around our house recently, I began thinking about how so many people I know are facing long challenges they aren't sure they can endure. Some received a diagnosis that says they have to battle disease for the rest of their lives. Some long to be married, but have not found that special someone. Some are out of work and haven't landed a job they love. Some long to have kids but still struggle with infertility. For some, it's been months. For others, years or even decades.

Waiting is not new for believers. Joseph of Old Testament fame had to wait about 13 years for the God-given dream about his family recognizing his leadership to come true. Joshua and Caleb had to traipse around the wilderness for 40 years to receive the land and victories God promised them. Scholars suggest it took Noah many years to build the ark that God promised would save his family and all the animals from destruction in the great flood. Then they had to stay on that boat for over a year from the time the raindrop first fell till the time when they could step out onto dry ground and start over.

We all go through times when we wonder how much longer our challenge is going to last. Each one of us wonders if we have enough left in our tank to make it through. If that's where you are in life right now, then let the lyrics below from *Fighter,* an old-school band who recorded them more than a quarter century ago resonate with you... let you know you're normal... and hopefully stir you to hope. Because God has made you strong enough, and He always keeps His promises!

Look me in the eye, and tell me I'm gonna make it
Look me in the eye, and promise an end to the story
Tell me that my heart is tough,
Tell me that I've faith enough
Look me in the eye

Scripture To Study: Habakkuk 1:12-2:3
Key Verse: "... wait patiently, for it will surely take place"
Prayer: *Heavenly Father, sometimes it feels like the challenge I am facing is too much to handle, like it will never be resolved. Please give me grace and patience till You come through for me. I love You, and...*

DAY 118
RAT-DOG BECOMES TEACHER

We have a dog. A Schnauzer to be exact. For those who don't know their doggie pedigree history, Schnauzers were originally bred in Europe to serve on farms as "rat dogs." They have wicked-quick reflexes and speed. Their sense of sight is amazing, and they will go after their prey with intense focus.

That's a good thing for us because we hate lizards in our family. We're not afraid of lizards, mind you. Just basically disgusted by them.

So you can imagine our consternation when a decent-sized lizard bolted in the door as I was shutting it recently. The boys jumped up and hollered, "Lizard, lizard!" I looked down, spotted it and began the hunt to evict it from our house.

I thought I had it trapped for a moment. Until I didn't. It was time to bring in the big gun, Sugar the Schnauzer. Soon she was in the game. We could tell that she saw it and was following it all over. Then, it underestimated her. It bolted, she flashed. Before we knew it, she had caught that lizard in her mouth. She grabbed it and locked down enough to kill it. We were elated. Eventually it quit moving, and Sugar dropped it, proud as could be.

You should have seen her. She was in her element. She was vibrant, alive, excited and energetic. It was obvious she was doing what she was created to do. She was living in her purpose.

That's what life should be like for each of us, full of passion and energy. When we live in the purpose for which we were created, the world springs into full-color. Jesus said the enemy of our souls comes to steal, kill and destroy, but that Jesus came to give us a full, abundant life. You have a purpose. Connect with God, and pursue it.

Take a lesson from Sugar "the rat-dog." Live in your purpose! Go after what energizes you. Go after your God-given purpose, and you will live a full life, making a significant impact on this world!

Scripture To Study: John 10:6-10
Key Verse: "My purpose is to give them a rich and satisfying life."
Prayer: *Jesus, I want to live in my purpose like You lived in Yours. I want to live that abundant life You have given me. I love You, and...*

DAY 119
YOU HAVE NO CLUE

Recently, one of our boys was having a bad night. Well, at least he *felt like* it was a bad night. Things weren't going the way he wanted them to, and it was really frustrating him. We pressed on through "Bummerville," tucked the boys in bed, read the Bible, kissed them goodnight, and prayed. He went to bed thinking that life wasn't going all that great. Before going to sleep, he even mentioned that the next day was probably not going to be so great either.

What he didn't know was that we had already made fun plans for the next day that he was really going to enjoy. We had set activities up to do together as a family that were going to make his day great, but he had no clue. He was so focused on how bad things looked at the moment that he wasn't thinking about the potential for a better tomorrow. He didn't know that loving parents were making plans specifically to make his life great.

Most of us are not so different. We sometimes forget that we have a Heavenly Father who loves us deeply and who has made plans for us... plans for good and not for disaster, to give us future and a hope (Jeremiah 29:11).

All we see is our current situation and how bleak life looks to us at the moment. We can hardly imagine a brighter, better tomorrow. We don't envision a scenario in which our life goes from what seems difficult to what will be delightful.

Little do we know, our Father has set up activities specifically designed for our joy and pleasure. If we would just stop and ask Him, He might not give us all the details, but He might just tell us to cheer up because we are going to love what He has in store for us tomorrow.

Why not stop right here, right now and ask Him about tomorrow? It might take the edge off whatever has you discouraged today. Try it. You'll be glad you did!

Scripture To Study: Jeremiah 29:10-14
Key Verse: "For I know the plans I have for you..."
Prayer: *Father, I know You love us and have good things in store for us. I look forward to what You have waiting. I love You, and...*

DAY 120
PLANS

One of my favorite movie quotes is also one of the most ridiculous ever. It comes from the animated movie *Turbo,* about a snail who wants to be a racer. An elderly woman who helps sponsor the taco vendor helping the nitro-infused snail race human-size cars says to him, "You got a plan, Taco Man?"

Good parents plan for their kids to do good things. They believe in their kids. They support their kids. They set their kids up to do good in this world, and God is the best Parent ever. God wants us to do good things. He even expects us to do good things.

How do I know? Ephesians 2:10 tells us God made us masterpieces so that we can do the good things He planned for us long ago. How long ago? *Long* ago! Like before you were born. Before the world was created. Before time was even kickstarted. And Psalm 139:16 tells us, "Every day of [your] life was recorded in [His] book. Every moment was laid out before a single day had passed."

God has a plan He knows can bring the greatest fulfillment to us and make the greatest impact through us on this world, but He doesn't force it on us. Yet, when we go along with His plan, we are assured of success.

When Noah went along with God's plan, his family and animals of every kind were rescued. When Moses went along with God's plan, an entire nation was freed from slavery. When David went along with God's plan, Goliath was permanently hushed.

What would happen tomorrow if today we got on-board with God's plan for us to do the good things He set us up for? Perhaps human trafficking would be ended. Or orphans would be adopted into forever families. Or college scholarships would be funded. Or the hungry would be fed. Or a cure for a disease would be discovered.

Let's get on-board with God's plan today and see what He does. You can be sure He has something great in store!

Scripture To Study: Ephesians 2:8-10
Key Verse: "He has created us... so we can do the good things He planned for us long ago."
Prayer: *Dear Lord, I want what You want. I trust Your plan for my life is best. I want to make a difference for You. I love You, and...*

DAY 121
YOU'VE BEEN SET UP

Whether you realize it or not, you've been set up. Someone has been laying out an intricate, detailed plan which directly affects you. The good news is that it's God. The rest of the good news is that He loves you, and it is things to benefit you that He has been scheming.

Psalm 139:16 reads, "You saw me before I was born. Every day of my life was recorded in Your book. Every moment was laid out before a single day had passed."

Jeremiah 29:11 points out, "'For I know the plans I have for you,' says the Lord. 'They are plans for good and not for disaster, to give you a future and a hope.'"

And Ephesians 2:10 declares, "For we are God's masterpiece. He has created us anew in Christ Jesus, so we can do the good things He planned for us long ago."

God is not sitting in Heaven figuring out how He can punish you. He is working all things together for your good (Romans 8:28). He has created a plan to bless you. To help you. To prosper you. To propel you. To give you life to the fullest.

John, the disciple who was probably closer relationally to Jesus than any other on this planet, recorded Jesus' words in John 10:10, "...My purpose is to give them a rich and satisfying life."

You see, you've been set up. No, not by me. But you've been set up by God to succeed. To thrive. To flourish. To make a difference in this world. To impact others. To create. To dream. And as a result, to be drawn closer to Him in love.

Why not stop right now and take a moment to recognize Him and His amazing plan for you. Pause to thank Him, to let Him know that you appreciate Him, and maybe even to ask what other good plans He has for you?

Scripture To Study: Psalm 139
Key Verse: "Every moment was laid out before a single day had passed."
Prayer: *Lord, thank You for Your spectacular plan for my life. I simply accept it and come into agreement with it today. I love You, and...*

DAY 122
YOU CAN'T LOSE

For those who love an intriguing story, check out Joshua chapter one in Scripture. It's the sixth book in. Moses, the great hero of the Old Testament Scriptures, has died, and it has fallen to his apprentice Joshua to lead millions of Jews at least half his age into the land God had promised to give them.

No big deal... you know, overthrow entire nations, defeat multiple armies, keep millions of your people united as you conquer new territory. Just an average day for most of us, right? Yeah, not for Joshua either. So God sends an angelic messenger to reassure Joshua that God pays for what He orders. That is, if God told Joshua *to* do it, then He was going to make sure Joshua *could* do it.

The Amplified version turns the phase this way... "Have not I commanded you? Be strong, vigorous, and very courageous. Be not afraid, neither be dismayed, for the Lord your God is with you wherever you go." Basically, God is telling Joshua, "You can't lose!" Joshua followed the Lord's command, and God gave Joshua success.

Now we could be tempted to think this is a neat story from thousands of years ago, which has no bearing on our lives today, but nothing could be further from the truth. The God who commanded Joshua, and then came through for Joshua to succeed at fulfilling that command, wants to be active in our lives in the same way today! He calls us to go after some massive undertaking for Him, and whatever He asks of us, He stands ready, willing and able to make sure we succeed at it.

So, what is it that He has commanded you? Is it to forgive someone? Or launch a business which will help people in poverty? Run for political office? Start a non-profit to help couples struggling with infertility be able to afford to adopt? Whatever it is that God has asked of you, you need to know... You can't lose!

Scripture To Study: Joshua 1
Key Verse: "Have I not commanded you?"
Prayer: *Heavenly Father, I accept the massive challenge You are calling me to conquer today for Your Kingdom. I will obey You, follow Your plan and trust You to make it work out. I love You, and...*

DAY 123
THE WHOSOEVERS

I love that Jesus came to the lowly. He came to Mary, a young woman, probably 13-15 years old. Women were often considered citizens of lower rank than men in biblical times. God didn't let the gender He gave her keep Him from coming to her, and He didn't let the fact that she was young keep Him from choosing her to play a major role in Christ's incarnation.

God also chose to come to the shepherds. Not just any shepherds either. No, the low guys on the totem pole of the shepherd hierarchy. The guys who were lowly enough that they got stuck with the night shift. Sure it was an important task... an important task no one really wanted to do. Yet God chose to send angels to them and inform them first of Christ's arrival. He chose to make them the first evangelists and missionaries carrying the good news to everyone they could find to tell.

Isn't it interesting, though, that God is not only interested in the lowly. Oh no! He cares deeply about the lofty as well. The night Christ was born, He set a star in the sky for the rich, wise and powerful kings from the east to see and pursue.

He may have reached out to the lowly, but He also attracted the lofty. All who met Jesus back in those first years of His childhood & youth understood that He was someone extraordinary. They gravitated to Him. They were drawn to Him.

Believe it or not, He is still attracting crowds of followers from the lowly to the lofty today... at least when they really meet Him and not some warped misrepresentation of who He truly is.

Today, whether you consider yourself lowly or lofty, join in the celebration! Celebrate with all those who bow their knee, worship Him, and spread the good news about Him wherever they go!

Scripture To Study: Luke 2:8-20
Key Verse: "The shepherds went back to their flocks, glorifying and praising God for all they had seen and heard."
Prayer: *Lord, thank You for looking past those things others might judge me by, and loving me simply for me. I love You, and...*

DAY 124
PICK THE RIGHT INSTRUMENT

When I walked into the upstairs room of the church on the last Wednesday night of the year, I was greeted immediately by the rich, deep tones of a double bass being played by a teenager. His name is Bryan, and what sounded like beautiful music to me, I later discovered was Bryan simply warming up to play with the team which would lead worship that evening in the service.

I spoke to the group that night, and when our time together was over, I headed for Bryan to pepper him with questions about how long he has played, and what he wants to do with his talent. He has played for years and would love to play in that major city's Symphony.

Then I asked a question out of ignorance. I assumed different basses were made from different types of wood, and I wondered if different types of wood caused the instrument to sound different. Bryan said, "Oh, yeah. This is an inexpensive rental made of laminate, but some are made of maple or other woods. Each one plays differently, so you have to pick the one that's right for you. Each person has an instrument that is right for them." He said price and quality do not determine what makes an instrument right for a person. He told me he had even tried a $20,000 bass once, but it wasn't right for him.

Bryan's description of how the instrument and the musician must be right for each other reminded me of Romans 12:6... "In His grace, God has given each of us gifts for doing certain things well."

God has just the right gift for each of us in life which will make us seem as masterful to others as Bryan seemed to me that night. Whether engineering or encouragement, baking or biology, homemaking or history-making, God has a gift just right for you. He has a situation and location just right for you.

Bigger isn't always better. "Better" isn't always better. Put your gift with the right instrument, and we will all enjoy listening to you play the song of your life... even when you're just warming up.

Scripture To Study: Romans 12:1-8
Key Verse: "In His grace, God has given us different gifts..."
Prayer: *Lord, please help me to use the gifts you have given me in the way You say is best. I want to bless others and You. I love You, and...*

DAY 125
MESSY WORKSHOPS

I have almost successfully converted our open garage into a woodworking shop. Yet, no matter how frequently I sweep the floors and pick up all the scrap pieces, there is sawdust everywhere. Even though we try to keep it neat, it never seems fully clean and tidy. Yet, it is a workshop. It's not designed to show off tools. There are stores and websites for that. Instead, this is where the beauty that was once an idea becomes reality.

Beautiful results can come out of messy workshops. In fact, they often do. Painters' studios have splatters. Flower shops have clippings. Automakers' production facilities have metal shavings and grease. We all see the finished works... the gorgeous arrangement, the piece of art, the furniture in the showroom, the sleek vehicle on the commercial, and we fail to notice the messiness it took to produce them.

Sometimes we do the same with our lives... or the lives of those we know. We want to see a finished product, a piece of art. We want to see it all dusted off, trimmed, adjusted, placed in perfect lighting and accented to highlight its magnificence, but we fail to notice that life is produced in messy workshops. We can each produce beautiful results from the workshops of our lives, but it might be a messy process.

That's okay. Solomon said in Proverbs 14:4, "Without oxen a stable stays clean, but you need a strong ox for a large harvest." In other words, you can have a neat, pretty, little life that everyone oohs and ahhs at, but in order to truly get anything accomplished which benefits others, there's probably going to be a mess to be cleaned up from time to time.

Something beautiful and wonderful is being crafted in you. It won't be long, and people will look at what you produce and stand in awe. There may be a mess all over the place right now, but that just means there is some serious work going on, and something beautiful is being made. Stay at it. We can't wait to see what is produced in you!

Scripture To Study: Proverbs 14:4
Key Verse: "...you need a strong ox for a large harvest."
Prayer: *Dear Lord, help me deal with the mess made in creating something beautiful in my life... and in the lives of others. I love You, and...*

DAY 126
PUTTING OUT BIRDSEED

For the second time that winter, we had snow! That is probably not a big deal for those of you who don't live in the Deep South, but for those of us who do... it's a pretty awesome. Interestingly, this time with the snow, we saw a significant number of songbirds gathering around our property in their search for food. There were cardinals, bluebirds, finches and wrens. It was so fun to just sit and watch them.

Alex remembered we had some birdseed and decided to put some in a feeder hanging from our front entryway. He filled it up, and then spread some on the ground as well. Soon the birds found the seed, and they haven't stopped coming. Knowing we helped them and seeing how excited they are about this provision has made our bird watching even that much more enjoyable.

Now, those birds didn't know where they were going to find food. They didn't ask for the food. They didn't knock on our door to see if we had any birdseed. They were simply searching. We saw their need. We had the ability to provide. We cared enough to help them.

As I thought about that, I recalled what Jesus said in Matthew 6:26, "Look at the birds. They don't plant or harvest or store food in barns, for your Heavenly Father feeds them. And aren't you far more valuable to Him than they are?"

I don't know what you need today, but God does. He's watching, and He will provide. When He does, He will enjoy watching as you take in His blessings. Blessings you could not obtain on your own, which you did not know were coming, and which were lovingly provided by Someone greater than you.

I promise, you are more important to God than the songbirds around our home. Yet God made sure a nine-year old put out birdseed for them, and He will make sure that your needs are provided for as well! Now, keep your eyes open... He's putting out birdseed for you today!

Scripture To Study: Matthew 6:25-33
Key Verse: "Look at the birds... your Heavenly Father feeds them."
Prayer: *Heavenly Father, I choose to trust You and not worry today. I will believe that You see my needs and will provide. I love You, and...*

DAY 127
EXPLAIN THAT

The word of the day on my Merriam-Webster app is "retrodict." That was a new one for me. It's a verb that means, "to use new information to explain the past." Wouldn't that be handy? I'd love to be able to explain some of the things that have happened to me in the past. For example, we couldn't understand why God wasn't answering our prayers for our international adoption to go through... until years later when God miraculously gave us two sons biologically.

That has to be the way Joseph felt as he trekked over 400 miles across the wilderness to Egypt, having been sold by his brothers to some passing slave traders. Or as he sat in an Egyptian jail, falsely accused of attempted rape. Or when he remained in jail after helping one of Pharaoh's prominent servants who promised he would help get Joseph out, but forgot. It couldn't have made sense at the time. He probably wondered why God would let this happen? What about his dreams? The ones God had given him?

It wasn't until Joseph had interpreted Pharaoh's troubling dream, had been named second in command of the most powerful nation on the earth at the time, rescued that nation, and his brothers knelt before him begging for food to save their family that Joseph was able to retrodict... to use new information to explain the past. In Genesis 50:20, Joseph tells his brothers that though they meant to harm him, God intended to use that to save their families' lives, and thus fulfill the dreams He had given Joseph as a teenager.

Maybe today you can't explain the stuff that has gone wrong in your life. Don't give up. Keep being your best. Keep trusting God and honoring Him. There *will* be a day when He gives you new information which will make it possible for you to interpret, understand and explain what has happened to you in the past. One day, it will all make sense. Until then, let it be enough to know that day is coming, and God is with you all along the way.

Scripture To Study: Genesis 50:14-21
Key Verse: "... but God intended it all for good."
Prayer: *Lord, I don't understand why I am having to go through all this, but I know You have a plan. Stay with me. I love You, and...*

DAY 128
KNOWN

I love walking outside on a clear, cool night and gazing into the dark sky full of stars. It's even better seeing the first star or two appear, and then watching as the sky populates almost magically with so many stars they cannot be counted. On a night like that, it's easy to begin to feel slightly minuscule. The enormity of the universe with all those stars has the ability to help us put ourselves in perspective. But if we're not careful, we can begin to think we are so small that we are overlooked. Lost. Unknown. Yet nothing could be further from the truth.

The prophet Isaiah wrote, "Look up into the heavens. Who created all the stars? He brings them out like an army, one after another, calling each by its name. Because of His great power and incomparable strength, not a single one is missing."

Think about that for a moment. Those stars are known. God, who created them, knows each of their names, and calls their names every 24 hours. They are personal to Him, unique enough to have their own name. And not a single one of them ever goes missing. He always knows their location. They never escape His sight. He knows where they are at every moment, even when you and I don't see them.

Here's the thing... you are far more important to God than any of His other creations, like stars. So you can be sure that, since *they* are known to Him, *you* are even more so known to Him. Today— every day— He knows your name and calls your name. You never get out of His sight. He always knows right where to find you.

You are known. The next time you forget that, or are tempted to think it's not true... walk outside, look up into the night sky, and remember you are more known than any one of those beautiful stars you see. In that moment, open your heart and mind, and listen closely, because He will come alongside you and whisper your name as well.

Scripture To Study: Isaiah 40:26-31
Key Verse: "He brings them out... calling each by its name."
Prayer: *Sovereign Lord, You know everything. Since You know the stars by name and call them each by their name, I trust You know me and will be close to me each day. Thank You! I love You, and...*

DAY 129
BIG BROTHERS

In 1981, Angela's family moved from Georgia to Louisiana. Angela was in first grade, and adjusting to a new school was hard enough, but then she started having less to eat for lunch each day. One afternoon, she came home from school hungry, and asked her mom why she had only packed her half a sandwich for lunch. When Mama informed her that she had packed her a *full* sandwich *and* other food, they realized something was afoot. They did a little research and soon discovered a little boy in Angela's class had been sneaking food from her lunchbox each day.

Her parents tried everything they could do to help her deal with the problem. They informed the teacher. They coached her to watch her lunchbox, but still tears came each day at school time.

That is, until her big brother, Tim, who just happened to be in tenth grade, took matters into his own hands. Tim is fairly reserved, but he had had enough of his little sister being bullied. So, one morning as he drove her to school, he told her, "You tell that little boy that your big brother says if he bothers you today or messes with your lunch, in the morning when he sees this old yellow truck coming, he better run and hide!"

Guess what... No more tears! Angela was emboldened. She realized her adversary had been outsized, outsmarted and outmatched. Simply hearing Tim speak those words gave her the strength and confidence she needed each day going forward. She knew all she had to do was mention it to Tim, and he would set the situation right.

Similarly, each Christian has a big Brother in Jesus Christ. Scripture calls Him "the first-born" and "our older brother." He said in John 16:33 that when we have problems in life, we can relax because He has overcome this world. Are you facing a challenge today it seems you can't overcome on your own? Take a moment to let your Big Brother know, and when the enemy of your soul sees Him coming, he had better run and hide!

Scripture To Study: John 16:33
Key Verse: "But take heart, because I have overcome the world."
Prayer: *Jesus, I am so glad You are my big Brother! I need You to come to my rescue and solve my problem for me. I love You, and...*

DAY 130
WHAT'S YOUR "ONLY?"

It's so easy for us to see our own faults, flaws and limitations. For example, when I play basketball, I am acutely aware that I am only 5'8" tall. Without assistive eyewear, I can see clearly that I can't even read the "E" on the top of the Snellen chart in the optometrist's office. When I look at the balance in our checking account, I understand our spending limitations.

We all have stuff we're not capable of on our own. That doesn't mean, though, that it is impossible for us to achieve something greater than we can in the natural. Check out what God said to the Jewish people through His prophet Isaiah, "Yes, think about Abraham, your ancestor, and Sarah, who gave birth to your nation. *Abraham was only* one man when I called him. *But when I blessed him, he became* a great nation."

Abraham was only one guy. He and his wife struggled with infertility. Yet God said they would be the ancestors of many people. God extended that promise to say their descendants would be as numerous as the stars in the sky or the grains of sand on the seashore... in other words, too many to count. Abraham's "only" was that he was only one old guy. Sarah's "only" was that she barren. But when God blessed them, generations... people groups... whole nations began. Abraham was "only" one man, but when God blessed him, he became more.

What's your "only" today? What's that thing that limits you, which you think prevents you from being all that God says you can, should and will be? Is it your age? Is it your health? Is it your education? *You* may be limited by your "only," but God is not. When God blesses you, you become whatever He is capable of making you.

So, go ahead. State your "only." That will just show how big the miracle really is when God blesses you and you become more than you could on your own.

Scripture To Study: Isaiah 51:1-3
Key Verse: "But when I blessed him, he became..."
Prayer: *Lord, I may not seem like much to myself or others, but You can do anything. Make something great out of me. I love You, and...*

DAY 131
JESUS WAS SAD

Each night, we sit next to the boys' beds and read a Bible story from each of their Bibles, and then we pray together as a family before they go to sleep. One night recently, Angela was reading in Austin's Bible about the Passion week. She read what the Scriptures say about Jesus in the Garden of Gethsemane from Mark 14:32-42. Along the way in his study Bible, there are little one-line commentary thoughts and activities that go along with the story.

Angela read these words aloud, "Jesus was sad, so He prayed." When she said it, I was struck. I have times when I'm sad. I mean, I'm normally pretty upbeat, but I have my own moments of melancholy. In fact, I had an afternoon and evening when sadness hit me out of nowhere not so long ago. I couldn't pin-point its cause. I was just sad.

When Jesus was at what was probably the saddest moment of His life on this planet, He chose to talk with His Heavenly Father about what was going on and how it was making Him feel. He took His sadness to the One who could actually do something about it. In the end, God didn't change the situation, but He did strengthen Jesus to be able to endure it. The emotional, physical and spiritual suffering Jesus faced over the next 24 hours seems almost incomprehensible. Yet in His sadness, He kept the conversation going with His Father, and He made it through the difficult times to the victorious times.

When you're sad— deeply sad, depressed, or grieving a loss— it can feel like nothing will help. When you don't know what else to do... when you don't think anything or anyone can help... do what Jesus did. Have a conversation with God, and invite Him to get involved in your life. Even if He doesn't change the situation— although sometimes He does— you will at least gain the strength you need to make it through the dark Fridays of despair on your way to the bright Sundays of hope!

Scripture To Study: Mark 14:32-42
Key Verse: "He became deeply troubled and... He prayed..."
Prayer: *Lord, it helps me to know that You were sad because I know You understand. Thank You for setting the example of how to handle my sadness through prayer. I love You, and...*

DAY 132
HOPE

I haven't always been the most mechanically savvy guy. Although, in the last several years, YouTube has really come through for me. Until recently, if something mechanical broke, I typically gave up on it after about five minutes of tinkering, and determined that I had to go buy a new one. or just do without. But I've learned that carburetors can be cleaned out and a weed-eater resurrected (with my father-in-law's help.) Extension cords can have the shorted wires cut out and a new connection added to bring them back to usability. A cracked plastic "T" in a heater hose can be replaced by a brass one and that system revived to make a minivan safely drivable again.

It's funny how something so small can produce hope. It makes me believe that, if *those* things were able to be revived and resurrected, maybe I don't have to give up on other broken things.

That's the message of Christ rising from the dead... hope through resurrection. When Jesus rose from the dead, He conquered fear, despair, and the unknown. Jesus' resurrection said to those who follow Him that they can have real, genuine, authentic hope. It took some of them a little longer to accept that He was really alive and that they could hope again, but when they encountered the resurrected Savior, hope sprung to life anew in their hearts.

The resurrection of Jesus Christ says that, since He could come back from being dead, there is hope that other things in our lives which have died can also be resurrected. Dead relationships in marriage or between parents and children can live again. Health can be resurrected. Finances can be resurrected. Dreams can be resurrected.

Is there something dead in your life today that needs to be revived? In the midst of despair and loss, hope can turn things around and bring them back to life. Today, give whatever it is to the One who brings hope to each situation from an empty tomb!

Scripture To Study: Luke 24:1-12
Key Verse: "He isn't here! He is risen from the dead!"
Prayer: *Jesus, I am so grateful that You are alive. I accept that what is dead in me can be resurrected by Your power. I love You, and...*

DAY 133
FIGURING IT ALL OUT

When our boys know we are going on vacation, they try to figure out all the details of the trip. They want to know when we will leave, which route we are taking, if we will stop at places we have stopped before, where and what we will eat, where we will stay, who will sleep where, if they will get to do the things they want to do, which clothes they will need, what will happen if weather messes up our plans, how they will pay for souvenirs, when we will leave to come home, etc. They want to figure it *all* out.

As amazing, smart, and resourceful as our boys are, though, I don't think they could plan out our vacation. They don't know how to route travel, book lodging, buy food for meals, secure tickets for activities, fuel up the vehicle, or any of the other details to pull off a great trip. They should let us handle the details, and just enjoy.

So we tell them we have taken care of all of the details necessary for the trip to be successful, and yet, this doesn't always satisfy them. They want to figure it all out. We just want them to relax, look forward to the trip, enjoy the journey and accept what we have planned.

It is so crystal clear to me as an earthly dad that I will work out the details in a way that is best and will bless my kids, and yet I sometimes treat my Heavenly Father the same way my boys treat me. I expect Him to tell me all the details before I would need to know them. I try to figure it all out instead of trusting Him fully. I ask Him about all the same details, even as He reassures me He has it under control.

Jesus spoke to this very issue when He said that we don't need to worry about tomorrow, that our Heavenly Father knows what we need, and He will take care of all the details in our lives.

So, let's relax and look forward to what God has in store for us. Let's quit trying to figure out how He is going to get us from where we are to where need to be. He's got this! And it is going to be a great journey!

Scripture To Study: Matthew 6:25-34
Key Verse: "So don't worry about these things..."
Prayer: *Heavenly Father, today I choose to quite worrying about the details of life and leave them to You. I trust You fully. I love You, and...*

DAY 134
GARAGE SALE LIFE

PR31 and I love a good garage sale... both shopping at them and having them. We were talking recently about how certain items ought to be priced when having a garage sale, and she said to me, "Isn't it crazy that pieces of your life can reduced to placing a sticker on them, and selling them for 25 cents?" That totally caught my attention. We talked about how items which we once felt were so important in our lives, we are now more than willing to part with as if they didn't matter to us at all. We decide whether to sell or even trash them.

I've been thinking about that throughout the day, and I'm reminded of how Jesus says in Matthew 6 that we should focus our attention on what really matters in life... those things that are going to last into eternity. He says we should store up treasures in Heaven where they cannot be taken, or destroyed, or— in my translation— sold for a quarter at a garage sale.

In the long run, people are what matter. Relationships matter. Kindness, love and respect matter. Generosity and grace matter. Feeding the hungry, healing the hurting, and helping the poor matter. Taking care of widows and orphans matters. None of those would ever be sold for 25 cents at a garage sale, and they just might generate some interest in your account in Heaven.

So before you buy that thing you just can't live without today, ask yourself how much you'll probably sell it for in a garage sale five or ten years from now. When this season's hot fashion trend is then a fashion faux pas... or that latest technology is totally outdated and no longer supported by most devices... will it really matter that you had it?

I'm not against having cool stuff. I'm just more in favor of making sure I keep my priorities right. I want to stockpile treasures in Heaven instead of just getting a quarter for something at a garage sale.

Scripture To Study: Matthew 6:19-21
Key Verse: "Store your treasures in Heaven..."
Prayer: *Lord, please help me keep my heart and my bank account focused on eternity. I want to store up treasures where it matters most, with You. I want to invest in people, not stuff. I love You, and...*

DAY 135
THE BIG BOOK OF TEARS

You might think that because I'm an author, I love to read. I do read. It's just that it takes me a long time to read because I process as I read. I can't just skim a book to gain the major points, set it aside, and move on. So, I'm super selective about what I choose to read, even the length of a book. Too many pages, and I just get bogged down. Apart from the Bible, most books I choose to read are 200 pages or less.

I've never read *War and Peace*, and the rest of that story is that I do not plan to do so. Nor do I plan to read books with multiple volumes and thousands of pages. Still, I was intrigued when reading Scripture one day to find that God has a big book, and you might be surprised to find what He writes in His "Big Book."

For example, God has a *Big Book of Tears*. Psalm 56:8 says, "You keep track of all my sorrows. You have collected all my tears in Your bottle. You have recorded each one in Your book."

Of all the things God could write in His "Big Book," He chose to record your every tear... and mine. Most of us want to forget most of the tears we have cried in life, but God chooses to record those experiences for eternity. Why would He do that? He does it for two reasons:

- He wants us to know that He knows... and cares. God keeps a record of our tears to let us know that He is "touched with the feeling of our infirmities" (Hebrews 4:15), and...

- He is keeping track of everything the enemy of our souls has done to cause us sadness and pain so that He can bring him to account for those actions, and bless us for the times when we have been mistreated. Isaiah tells us that God will restore to us double for our trouble, and He has the accounting records to settle that score accurately.

If life has brought you to tears today, just know that He knows, He cares, and He is going to set things right. Now that's one big book that might just be worth reading!

Scripture To Study: Psalm 56:8
Key Verse: "You have recorded each one in Your book."
Prayer: *Dear Lord, thanks for taking note of my sorrows in life so that you can set things straight and repay me. I love You, and...*

DAY 136
STRETCHED

When I was a kid, I thought Stretch Armstrong was one of the coolest toys in existence. To my small arms, it seemed like he could be stretched as far as I wanted. His arms stretched. His legs stretched. It was like there were no limits to his ability to be stretched. But as I grew up, I came to learn that Stretch Armstrong had his limits. People pushed him to his limits to see how far he could actually stretch. In fact, they stretched him till he snapped.

We can all be tempted to see ourselves as human versions of that toy... only able to stretch so far, and then break. We deal with hurts. Stretch. We care for an ailing loved one. Stretchhhh a little further. Financial challenges come along. Strrrrrreeeetttccch-hh. Soon, we feel like we cannot be stretched anymore... that if one more pressure in life tugs at us, we will snap in two and all our stretchy insides will ooze out.

The Apostle Paul knew that feeling. He begged God to make the stretching stop more than once, but God told him he could be stretched further than he thought because it wasn't about Paul's ability to stretch. Instead, it was about God's grace inside him giving him the ability to stretch even more than seemed possible.

If you're going through a time of stretching... if you've even asked God to put an end to the stretching... and yet you continue to be stretched... if your bank account balance is shrinking... if your health isn't improving... if your relationship with that person continues to worsen... if your dreams aren't coming true... if you've prayed about it more times than you can count and it hasn't changed, know this....

You won't snap. His grace is enough, all you need. His grace gives you some more stretchiness. And then some more. And some more. And some more. Unending grace to stretch.

So, you can relax Stretch _____ (*fill in the blank with your last name*), because God has put the right stuff inside you to stretch as far as you need to stretch!

Scripture To Study: 2 Corinthians 12:1-10
Key Verse: "My grace is all you need."
Prayer: *Father, I don't know how much more I can take. I need Your grace. Make me as stretchable as You can. I love You, and...*

DAY 137
WRING IT OUT

Kids amaze me with their ability to connect dots between the spiritual and the natural with what seems like such ease. It happened with Austin a few nights ago. Angela was reading him the story of Gideon from his Bible. In the account from Scripture, an angel visits Gideon who is hiding to do his work because marauding raiders from the country next door keep crossing the border to attack, pillage and destroy the Israelites crops. The angel tells Gideon that he is a "mighty hero," and that God has selected him to lead the charge against the enemy country's army, giving God's people peace and prosperity once more.

The problem was, Gideon wasn't sure he was up to the task because he didn't have the pedigree or skill set. So, he asks God to show him a sign in order for him to accept this is really God. and they are really going to defeat the enemy. Gideon asks for God to make a piece of wool that he leaves out overnight to be soaking wet from dew and the ground all around it completely dry the next morning. God agrees, and the next morning Gideon finds exactly what he asked for. Scripture says the wool was wet enough that he wrung water out of it.

Enter Austin. Upon hearing this, Austin says, "Oh, like when we wring out the washcloth when I take a bath!" Angela confirmed that he had understood what Gideon had done and went on reading, but I was soon lost in thought. When Gideon wrung out that wool, it was proof to him that God was speaking... that God wanted to empower him... that God was for him... that God would come through for him.

You know, God *is* involved in your life. He knows what you're facing, and He wants to make you victorious. *He* will work the miracle. He'd just like to include *you* in the process. So, if you're one of us who sometimes struggles to believe for the miraculous, just remember ol' Gideon the next time you finish bathing, and wring it out!

Scripture To Study: Judges 6-7
Key Verse: "Mighty hero, the Lord is with you!"
Prayer: *Lord, sometimes I need just a little extra reassurance of Your power in my life. Please show me again. I love You, and...*

DAY 138
BLAME OR CREDIT?

Since you are human, I will assume you have faced hurt or unfair treatment in your life like the rest of us. You've probably been wounded by people who were supposed to be for you, supposed to be on your side. When that happens, it's normal to feel emotional pain, to feel betrayed, to wonder why this bad stuff is happening to you. At some point, we need to come to terms with the fact that sometimes bad things happen to good people. The question becomes... What will you do with the bad stuff that has happened to you in life?

In the book of Genesis, we read about someone who was done really wrong. His name was Joseph. God had given him big dreams, but his brothers hated him for them. They sold him into slavery and told their dad he died. Then, though he excelled as a slave, he was falsely accused of attempted rape and sent to jail. In jail, Joseph excelled, but was forgotten. Finally, Joseph interpreted a dream for the king and rose to second in command of Egypt. A famine ensued, and Joseph's brothers showed up to get food from Egypt where Joseph was in charge. Suddenly, Joseph was confronted with a choice. The very guys who had done him wrong were in front of him, and it was within his power to set things straight. In that moment, Joseph chose to give God credit instead of giving his brothers blame. Yes, they did bad things to him. He didn't ignore that fact. He just chose instead to focus on how God used the bad they had done to work for all their good.

The question before each of us today is the same one Joseph faced that day his brothers showed up... Will I choose to give God credit for His work, or will I choose to blame those who did me wrong?

God promises that He will set the record straight on our behalf, working out both the bad and the good for our benefit and His glory... *if* we will let Him. Let's choose to see how God has worked things out for our good and give Him credit. In the end, that's a winning choice!

Scripture To Study: Genesis 50:14-21
Key Verse: "...but God intended it all for good."
Prayer: *God, You and I both know I was done wrong. I trust You, and choose to give You credit for working it out. I love You, and...*

DAY 139
PEPPERS, PEOPLE AND PATIENCE

I am worse than our boys when it comes to waiting for plants in our garden to produce. I till the plot, and help pull the weeds. I help rake and hoe the rows. I may even help plant the seeds. Then we water... and wait. I know it will take a little while, but most of the plants grow so quickly to begin with that I get excited. At the sight of that first bloom, I know that a veggie or fruit is not far away... or so it seems.

This year, we planted red bell peppers. Right away, they took root, grew and put on blooms. The blooms have turned into big bell peppers... green bell peppers. One has grown so large that it began to bend the entire plant over, and yet it remains green.

We wondered why the peppers are not turning red, and so we did a little research. The problem, it would seem, is not with the plant but with me. Apparently, I am impatient. When the bell pepper is left to ripen to that full red color, it is sweeter to the taste, bringing full flavor and beautiful color to the meal. Also, by letting it fully mature, the pepper's vitamin levels increase multiplied times over, making it more beneficial to eat. But you have to wait for all of that.

Apparently, when it comes to waiting in my own life, I am again the problem. I am impatient. My Heavenly Gardener has placed me where He feels I will do best for the time being. He has made sure I have the right amount of what I need to thrive. I feel like I'm ready to be picked, but God says, "Wait. You're going to be even better. Just be patient. You will look better, taste better and be better."

I suppose we people are a lot like peppers. We require patience to reach maturity and be our best. Maybe that's why God said in His Word that, if we wouldn't give up, we would reap a harvest of blessing at the right time.

If you're not ripe, you're not ready. Be patient so you can be your best. The ripe time is the right time. Hang in there!

Scripture To Study: Galatians 6:7-10
Key Verse: "At just the right time we will reap..."
Prayer: *Holy Spirit, please gently help me to be patient. I want to be my best to honor You, even if I have to wait. I love You, and...*

DAY 140
PURE DELIGHT

I love that Scripture says in multiple places God delights in us. The Merriam-Webster dictionary defines delight as, "a high degree of gratification or pleasure; joy; also: extreme satisfaction."

Think about that for a moment. When God thinks about you, He smiles. He experiences a high degree of satisfaction and pleasure. He feels joy. He is extremely satisfied.

Ask yourself this question, and answer it honestly... Do you *really* view God as thinking and feeling that way about you? Or do you figure He's probably frustrated with you? Upset with you? Frowning or scowling at you?

How you view Him is important because it determines how you approach Him. If you think He's mad at you, you'll approach Him fearfully and with little hope of goodness from Him. But if you view Him as delighted over you, you'll approach Him with love and be confident that you will receive blessings from Him.

Too many people think God is mad at them and that He is looking for any little opportunity to punish them. He's not. He's looking for every opportunity to bless you... to bring that same delight, joy, pleasure and satisfaction to your heart which He experiences when He thinks of you.

Why not take this week— or if that's too much, then just start with this one day— and live determined to take God at His Word, viewing Him as delighted with you? When you think of Him, picture Him smiling as He says your name. Believe that He loves you and wants to give you good things for your life. Delight in Him like He delights in you.

I'm convinced that if you will change your perspective toward Him, you will find that life is much better as you live in His pure delight!

Scripture To Study: Psalm 37
Key Verse: "He delights in every detail..."
Prayer: *Lord, I smile to think that You smile when You think of me. That makes me feel so special, loved, and valued. I am determined today to take you at Your Word, and trust that you delight in me. I love You, and...*

DAY 141
THE STRUGGLE IS REAL

My Mom is a saint. For years— and by "years" I mean decades— she has battled physical challenges. Since my teens, I can remember her trying to overcome physical pain. Her heart. Her back. Her knee. Yet she doesn't complain. She cries sometimes. If we ask how she's doing, she might tell us as her family, but usually she just keeps on trooping through life despite it all.

The struggle is indeed real for her, and sometimes it's also really lengthy. Perhaps you're battling a lengthy struggle of your own today. Maybe it's a situation at work which only seems to get worse. Maybe you're trying to overcome depression, and it seems the battle will never end. Maybe you're enduring singleness, though you long to be married. Maybe you battle an addiction, though you long to be free. Or perhaps you struggle with infertility year after year as you watch others get pregnant and adopt multiple times.

Sometimes we pray and pray, only to have our challenge keep pace with us. Sometimes we plop down, and say, "I just can't take it anymore. When is this going to end?" J. Sidlow Baxter so eloquently captures this feeling with these words, "Perhaps at times we suffer more from the length than the strength of our trials."

Compared to others whose problems are worse than our own, it is easy to estimate the strength of our trial is not horrendous. We feel we could overcome it if the fight only lasted a few hours or a few days. But when that trial extends into weeks, months, years, and even decades, well... even a small trial endured over time can wear us down.

Please don't give up. You *are* going to make it. You *will* win if you make God the axle around which your life rotates. Jesus promised that He would be *with* us all the way to the end. So you're not going through this alone. Cry if you need to. Vent if you need to. That's normal. Then choose to get up tomorrow and go again, with the best attitude possible. You can do it!

Scripture To Study: Colossians 1:3-14
Key Verse: "... that you will be strengthened..."
Prayer: *Father, I am so tired. This challenge has been wearing me down. I need Your strength to keep going. I need You. I love You, and...*

DAY 142
MOMENTS THAT MATTER

I still remember more than 23 years later the pastors from Oklahoma where I had just begun as youth pastor driving almost nine hours to attend our wedding in Louisiana. They didn't have to, and I've never forgotten it. I still remember a decade later how so many friends brought our family food at the hospital every one of those first 41 days my Dad was there for a liver and kidney transplant. They didn't have to, and I've never forgotten. These were moments that mattered.

Recently, a dear friend and mentor had a critical health issue that landed him in the emergency room, and I was able to visit the hospital to check on him and his family before he had to be transported to another hospital hours away in another city. Then the next day, I was able to attend the funeral for the father of another friend. I could have passed on both opportunities. Neither was really convenient. Both took some rearranging of my schedule, but both were moments that mattered. The people for whom I made time each commented how much it meant that I had made the time and effort to be with them.

I'm not really good in either of those settings. I'm a little awkward. Even though I've been in vocational ministry for more than 2 decades, I still sometimes fumble with what to say that would be helpful and appropriate. Yet here's what is interesting... no one ever complains about— or even mentions— my faux pas.

That's because the power is in our presence, not our presentation. Simple, huh? Just show up. Just be there. Just value them and their feelings. Just put yourself in their shoes.

That's what God decided to do when He sent His only Son, Jesus, to come be Immanuel... God with us. He chose to walk a mile in our shoes. He chose to walk with us, talk with us, be with us. When we show up for someone else, we imitate Christ simply by our presence. Let's do our best to make the most of moments that really matter!

Scripture To Study: Philippians 2:1-11
Key Verse: "... take an interest in others, too."
Prayer: *Dear Lord, please help me today make time for people when it matters most, and help me to love them like You. I love You, and...*

DAY 143
FORGET THE FORECAST

It was raining outside at our house at that very moment. Why is that important? Well, when we checked the weather app that morning, like less than an hour earlier, it showed that there was a zero percentage chance of rain. In fact, it showed our weather would be sunny with temps getting up to 102 degrees. Yet, when we looked out the window, we saw clouds. Then, the rain just started falling.

We decided to ask Google Home if it was raining where we were. The artificial intelligence voice replied, "No, it is not raining where you are. It is sunny and 84 degrees." We tried two or three times, even using a zip code closer to our house than where it thinks we live. Same answer every time. Yet, we stood at the door, looking out at rain. Rain... on what was supposed to be a zero percent chance day. Rain... when there was no rain reported. It simply rained.

PR31 and I both went to each other simultaneously with the same thought... God can make something out of nothing. God can make something happen when the predictions and forecasts say it isn't going to happen. God can make something happen even when reports around clearly say it isn't happening. He doesn't need prognosticators to agree with Him. He doesn't need reporters to agree with Him. He can do what He wants... when He wants... out of nowhere.

When I think about this, I am reminded of the God written about in Romans 4:17 who calls things into existence that do not exist. He can do that in your situation. He doesn't need a prophet or a preacher to say it's going to happen. He doesn't even need anyone else to notice it's happening. He can make happen in your life what you need Him to make happen... even if it doesn't exist yet.

The God who calls things into existence which do not exist just made it rain at my house... and He will make something great happen in your life as well!

Scripture To Study: Romans 4:16-25
Key Verse: "God who... calls things into existence..."
Prayer: *God, You have all power and all authority. Work miracles in my life today. Create out of nothing in me. I love You, and...*

DAY 144
UNKNOWN PATHS

I have a friend who has worked for a major U.S. corporation for a number of years. Several months ago the company announced everyone working in his division would be let go before the end of the year. However, there would be three transitional jobs lasting a year and a half to help wrap everything up for the move of work to another country. So, my friend applied for the three jobs, along with about a hundred other workers.

The company said they would meet with people by the end of the month to let them know if they still had a job, and my friend's meeting finally came. We prayed God would give him favor and bless him with one of these jobs, but he only had a 3% chance of getting one.

In the meeting, the bosses began talking to him about work he wasn't familiar with. It sounded like they were talking as if he already had the job. They told him that the company didn't want to lose him, and so they were moving him to another division. His pay would remain the same, and he would retain his benefits. Also, this would be a job with their typical four-year contract. For the record, my friend needed 3½ more years to lock in healthcare for he and his wife throughout their retirement.

So basically, God gave my friend a job he never applied for, in which he lost no pay and kept all the benefits. God took his 3% chance, added 97% plus to it, and gave him something he didn't even know to ask for. It reminds me of Psalm 77:19 telling how God parted the Red Sea, giving the Israelites a way of escape from the pursuing Egyptians. The water parted, creating a completely dry path for them to cross through. The Psalmist calls it, "... *a path no one knew was there.*"

Maybe you're facing a situation today that seems impossible. Don't give in to fear and doubt. Instead, give your situation to God, and trust Him to come through for you. God has ways to answer your prayers that you haven't even thought to ask Him about... a path no one knows is there.

Scripture To Study: Psalm 77
Key Verse: "... a pathway no one knew was there!"
Prayer: *Lord, it is so reassuring to know that You have a way to work things out for me even when I don't see a way. I love You, and...*

DAY 145
WHY, LORD?

Maybe you've wanted to add children to your family and haven't been able to. Maybe you are battling an emotional issue you haven't been healed of yet. Perhaps you long to fulfill your purpose, but every door you knock on seems to be locked. Or maybe you long to be married, and it hasn't happened... even though you prayed.

When we come to times like this, it's easy to wonder, "Why? Why won't You answer my prayer, Lord? Why is it taking so long? Why aren't you coming to my rescue, Lord?"

The good news is that you are not alone. Scripture tells of two sisters and their brother who encountered their own "Why, Lord" moment. Lazarus got sick, and so his sisters asked Jesus to come heal him. They were good friends of Jesus. So they assumed He would come immediately when He heard Lazarus was sick and heal him like He had healed so many others.

But Jesus chose to wait two days before making the two-day walk to their home in Bethany. By the time Jesus arrived, Lazarus had died. In their minds, Jesus was too late, but He didn't have to be. It baffled the sisters that Jesus didn't do what Jesus normally did, and their hearts were flooded with that one emotionally draining query... "Why, Lord?" When they asked Him, He said it would give God more glory. What? How was their brother dying going to give God more recognition and praise? You probably know the weariness of that question. I know I do.

Then Jesus showed them. He raised Lazarus from the dead. Their pain was eclipsed by their joy, and John records that *many* people believed in Jesus because of this miracle.

Jesus loved them, but He did it differently than they expected. And when we can't understand why, at least we can rest in the truth that He loves us, and He has a better way. He will show up and go through it with us... all the way to the miraculous end!

Scripture To Study: John 11:1-44
Key Verse: "Lord, if only You had been here..."
Prayer: *Jesus, I may not understand why right now, but I do know You love me, and You will never let me down. I love You, and...*

DAY 146
SATISFACTION GUARANTEED

Alex turned ten at his last birthday, and suddenly we have a kid in double digits! To celebrate, I ate cake. Too much cake. How could I not? Like the climber who climbed the mountain, I ate it because it was there. And because I *love* food!

I like to think about what I'll snack on and what I'll have for lunch... while I'm eating breakfast. Meeting someone... How can we work food in? Celebrating something... What kind of food will we have? Road trip... What kind of snacks to take, and where to eat along the journey?

Of course, if I eat something, I get thirsty. My beverage of choice throughout most of the day is usually strong, black coffee. Except when I'm hot and tired from exercising or working in the yard. Then I crave water. Nothing else quenches thirst like water.

Hunger and thirst are cravings which are part of our existence as humans, but there are deeper desires in each of us which long to be satisfied. We all long to belong. To be loved. To be wanted. We each need to know we have purpose and meaning. Too often, we try to satiate these deep longings with surface supplies. We feel our heart rumble for love, and we turn to a human. We feel parched in our soul to belong, and we join a club. Yet these deep-seated desires and cravings can only truly be fulfilled by One Person. In Psalm 145:16, we read that when God opens His hand, He satisfies the cravings and longings and desires which reach out from deep within us to find fulfillment.

Stop and ask yourself right now... What is it you *really* long for? If you're honest with yourself and God, it's most likely much deeper than the requests we make of Him for finances or fiancées. So the next time your stomach growls or your throat is parched, let it remind you that there is One who is ready to open His hand and satisfy the deepest desires of your heart. And His offer is... satisfaction guaranteed!

Scripture To Study: Psalm 145
Key Verse: "... You satisfy the hunger and thirst..."
Prayer: *Dear Lord, I bring the deepest cravings of my soul to You to satisfy. Fill and quench me today as only You can. I love You, and...*

DAY 147
IN HIS HEART

The morning began with *Frosty The Snowman* playing while PR31 made pancakes in the shape of reindeer, stars, snowmen and Christmas trees. It was the kick-off to our new family tradition, our annual "Team A's Christmas In July" celebration!

The temps are in the mid-to-high 90's outside with humidity in 90%+ range, but we set up a tree, hung the stockings, placed a few decorations around the house, played Christmas carols, and started the Christmas movies on Hallmark Channel. Soon, it felt like it was cooling down to be the most wonderful time of the year in our house. Various Christmas cookies were baked throughout the week as we celebrated again the coming of our Savior as a human being so that God could be with us. Stockings were slightly filled with treats, and gifts were exchanged.

We don't go crazy with the gift-giving thing during this time. Instead, we each draw one name of someone in the family and work at focusing on that one person. Mama & Daddy may sneak a couple extra gifts under the tree for fun, but we try to keep it simple.

As we drew names that first day, I suggested we each make a list of gift ideas so whoever got our name would have some ideas. Angela reminded me that we didn't do lists last year, instead opting to each see how well we knew the person we were shopping for. That's when Austin piped up, "Yeah, we have that person's list in our hearts."

I don't know what you need the Lord to do for you today. Maybe you feel like you need to give Him a list so He will know what to do. The thing is, He knows you so well that He has a list in His heart as to what to give you, and it will be better than anything you could have asked for. So just trust Him today. And when you open the gift He gives you, you will be pleasantly surprised at how well He knows you!

Scripture To Study: James 1:16-18
Key Verse: "Every good and perfect gift..."
Prayer: *Heavenly Father, thank You for knowing me so well. I receive whatever blessings You choose to give me. I love You, and...*

DAY 148
DADDDDYYYY!

An amazing thing happens when you become a parent; your ears become tuned to the voice of your children. I can be caught up in woodworking, mowing, or writing, and when my boys holler, "Daddddyyyy," I come running. We might be standing around in a crowd of people talking after church when I hear one of them call me by that term of endearment. I can pick their voice out of all the other kids running around. And if one of them is ever hurt or scared and hollers for me, you've never seen me move so quickly or so determinedly to get to them. The call of my children stirs something in me that motivates me to act.

I have no problem understanding that when it comes to my kids needing their Daddy, but sometimes I forget that God— my Heavenly Daddy— is an even better Daddy than me. All I need to do is holler for Him... to call out that term of endearment... and I suddenly have His fullest attention.

I love that Jesus called out, "Daddy," from the garden of Gethsemane when He was facing the darkest time of His life. He's my hero, my life example, and if He cried, "Daddy," then I can, too. I also love that Paul writes in Romans 8:15 that because God has adopted us and made us His children, we now call Him, "Daddy." He then writes in Galatians 4:6 that because we are His children, God prompts us to call out "Daddy" to Him.

You may think God's busy doing something else today. That He is not paying attention to you. That He doesn't know where you're at or what's going on in your life. You may feel like He can't or won't stop what He's doing just for you. But I promise that if you will call out to Him today with a heartfelt, "Daddddyyy," He *will* come running to you, ready to help you, ready to scoop you up in His arms and give you the strength you need to face whatever it is you're facing!

Scripture To Study: Galatians 4:4-7
Key Verse: "...prompting us to call out, Abba, Father."
Prayer: *Daddy, thanks for always listening out for and hearing me. I need You today. Please wrap me in Your loving arms and help me. I love You, and...*

DAY 149
DON'T FORGET TO REMEMBER

There is a new roller coaster at Silver Dollar City in Branson, MO called *The Time Traveler*. It's a different take on the roller coaster experience because your car spins throughout the entire ride. So, you may be looking forward and see what's coming, but by the time you get to that point, you may be facing backward. The ride gives you the ability to see where you just were while you head to where you're going.

Alex and I rode this ride a few months ago when we were there. Unfortunately, Austin was just a couple inches shy of making the height requirement to ride, but he keeps measuring in hopes of riding it the next time we go.

We were talking about the ride the other day and how fun it is when Austin, in his ever-insightful way, spoke up about wanting to ride it and said, "Sometimes I look forward so much, I just want to be able to look back and see where I've come from."

Wow! This boy already knows the importance of something God has been trying to teach all of us for thousands of years; don't forget to remember. It's important to look back and see where God has brought us from. It's important to remember how He has come through for us time and time again.

God has done a lot of good for each one of us. He didn't have to. He doesn't owe us anything. He does it because He loves us and wants the best for us. And if we will take the moments provided as the car on our roller coaster life spins to look back where we've come from, we won't be tempted to worry as much about the plunges, twists and loops ahead of us.

So, if you have the opportunity to make your way to Silver Dollar City, be sure to ride *The Time Traveler*. But if not, at least on the the roller coaster of your life... Don't forget to remember all the good things God has done for you!

Scripture To Study: Joshua 4:1-8
Key Verse: "These stones will stand as a memorial... forever."
Prayer: *Dear Lord, thank You for all You have done in my life in the past. Please help me take time each day to recall those blessings, knowing You have more good in store for me. I love You, and...*

DAY 150
FORWARD FOCUSED

My friend grew up on a farm, and in order to plow straight rows, they would put a stake at the end of the field and drive the tractor with plowing discs in a straight line toward it, looking at that one fixed point the entire time. If they looked backward to see what they plowed, they could be thrown way off-course. If they looked to the side, they might only get a little off-course to begin with, but over a distance that small percentage misplaced would in the end mess up the whole field. The cool thing was that, after the first row was plowed straight by looking ahead at the fixed destination, the stake was no longer needed on successive rows. They simply needed to put the edge of the disc in the first row and run along it because they knew it was straight. As long as they did the first row right, the rest of the rows would be straight also. It's the power of looking straight ahead at your destination.

Our eyes are on the front of our face for a reason. Wherever we are looking is where our brain tells our body we will probably be heading. That applies in the physical, but it also applies to the rest of our life.

There is no need to look backward because what's done is done. We can't go back and change any of it. To look backward is to begin trying to move toward our past, and we never arrive at that destination because it is unreachable. It throws our life way off-course.

To look to our sides is to be distracted, and that can cause us to veer off our path. Even though it is barely noticeable at first, looking off slightly in life can cause big problems later on.

Let's look ahead of us. Let's fix our eyes on our destiny. Let's set a fixed point in our future and stay focused on moving straight toward it. No looking back. No glancing off at distractions to our sides. Look forward. And what follows will be as straight as that first row.

Scripture To Study: Proverbs 4:25-27
Key Verse: "Mark out a straight path..."
Prayer: *Heavenly Father, You have given me a marker to guide my path in life. Please help me to stay steadily focused on what You have set in front of me. Keep my life straight to the end. I love You, and...*

CONCLUSION

I hope the last 150 days during which you have used this devotion have drawn you into a deeper, more fulfilling, more consistent relationship with the Lord. It has been my experience that, as I have spent more time with the Lord each day, it has morphed from what began as a duty into what has become a delight. In fact, I look forward to that time spent alone with Him each morning, and if I miss it or it is cut short for some reason, I can tell the difference in my day.

Several years ago, when Alex was about six, he began waking up earlier in the morning. I would normally wake up most days around 6:00am to have my time alone with the Lord and begin my day. But when Alex began coming in the living room and crawling up in my lap wanting to play or watch television, I discovered it was cutting into my time alone with the Lord. So, I backed up my wake-up time. But he kept coming in earlier.

Now don't get me wrong. I cherish those moments spent holding him in my lap and loving on him. I will treasure them as long as I live. But I knew that I needed to crawl up in the Lord's lap and let Him love on me even more if I was going to be the man I needed to be.

Then I remembered that it was my parents who first introduced me to daily time spent in the Word and in prayer as a child at that kitchen table. It hit me that it was time for me to pass along to my sons what had been passed down to me.

I began to explain to Alex that when men of God in this family wake up that early, we spend time alone with the Lord. I also let him know that his Mama was awake in the other room having her own time alone with the Lord. We talked about what it could look like for him to begin to start his day with the Lord. I wasn't sure initially if it would connect with him, but he really caught it.

We began with a daily devotional book for kids that I would read to him. It had a Scripture that went with it, and it ended with a prayer. We would read that, pray together, and then he was allowed to do other things.

To make this happen and still have the amount of time I wanted to have alone with the Lord myself, it meant I had to back my wake-up time even further. But that was okay with me because I saw how disciplined Alex was becoming, and I wasn't going to miss out on my time alone with the Lord.

After about a year of this, Alex asked me one morning if it would be okay for him to read his devotion and pray by himself, like I did. I was one proud daddy! I told him that was perfectly fine, and it was actually supposed to be like that. It wasn't long after that he began to stop coming in the living room in the mornings. When I inquired as to why, I discovered that he was getting alone to read his devotions and pray before he came to join me.

To this day, a few years down the road from when he started, he is still consistently making time to get alone with God each day to read Scripture and a devotion, and to pray. Nobody forces him. Nobody reminds him. He has built it into his life. This past Christmas, he asked for a Bible like ours, one with all the words and not just stories or devotions. He's taking his relationship with the Lord seriously, and it makes this daddy's heart smile.

Not too long ago, Austin began to wake up earlier and come in the living room with me. This time, I still treasured our moments together, but I also knew I needed to be strategic with our time. Now, each morning he comes in and gives me a hug. Then, he goes over to the sofa, picks up his kids devotional which includes a Scripture and a prayer, and quietly starts his day with the Lord while I am finishing up my time alone with the Lord. It is catching traction with him as well.

Can the boys always tell me exactly what they read or what it meant? No, but in the last week, Austin has begun to be able to tell which part of Scripture his devotions were about and what the main point of the devotion was. Are they perfect at applying everything they've learned to their lives? No, but just today Alex told me about a Proverb he read which helped him realize he needed to change an area of his life. Am I as proud as any dad could possibly be that my sons are learning to walk with the Lord daily? You know I am!

THE UPSIDE

I know that forty years from now, if they will stay at this consistently, they will probably have a close, one-on-one, personal relationship with the Lord. They will look at life each day from a better perspective. They will be able to teach their kids about how to connect with God personally. And I will feel like a successful dad.

You know, if kids can do this, you can, too. You have made a stellar start using this book. Don't stop now. Keep it going, and soon— if you're not already— you will be looking at life every day from... *The Upside*!

ALLEN CHAPIN

PERSONAL THOUGHTS

ABOUT THE AUTHOR

Allen Chapin is the passionately committed husband to "PR31" (aka, Angela) whom he met at Southwestern Assemblies of God University, and to whom he has been happily married for more than 23 years. He is also the wildly proud dad of two sons, Alex and Austin.

He enjoys crafting his own natural peanut butter, fishing for crappie and bream on light tackle, 1980's nostalgia and watching NFL football.

He is also an ordained minister with the Assemblies of God and has served that fellowship in leadership roles in a variety of local churches, at one of the fellowship's premier universities, as a statewide director, and as a traveling speaker.

Other Writings

Allen's first book, *I Got A "D" In Leadership: Anyone Can Lead*, is a practical manual for understanding and effectively building leadership teams. It is available on Amazon.com.

Allen also authors a daily blog called "Up: Encouragement and Motivation for Living Up In An Often Down World" which can be found at allenchapin.com/blog.

Connect With Allen

To connect with Allen with comments, questions or invitations to speak, feel free to utilize the following:

Email:
achapin70@gmail.com

Facebook:
facebook.com/allenangelachapin

Twitter & Instagram:
achapin70

51007281R00100

Made in the USA
Columbia, SC
17 February 2019